Unladylike

Resisting the Injustice of

Inequality in the Church

Copyright Notice

Unladylike

Resisting the Injustice of
Inequality in the Church

By Pam Hogeweide

What Others are Saying

The hope of transforming organized religion rests largely upon the full and free self-expression of women. This would require confronting the woefully insufficient view of women and structural sexism or gender inequality characteristic of most religious traditions. It would further necessitate a vigorous effort to empower the participation and leadership of women in church, mosque and synagogue. And for any of this to happen it would require a person of great courage to speak out and take up such a calling so threatening to the status quo. That person is Pam Hogeweide, and I'm convinced that her book, *Unladylike: Resisting the Injustice of Inequality in the Church*, will help inspire, invigorate and recast the place and significance of women in Christendom. Weaving together her own personal experiences and the stories of others, Pam unpacks the issue of inequality in the church in a way in which you truly get it. I am excited about promoting this book among my divine nobody tribe!"

Jim Palmer, critically acclaimed *author of Divine Nobodies* and *Wide Open Spaces,* and upcoming book, *Being Jesus in Nashville*

***

In *Unladylike* Pam Hogeweide employs her engaging tell-it-like-it-is style as she honestly and openly writes of her experience as a woman in the church world - from bumping up against the so-called stained-glass ceiling to being pressured into suppressing her God-given intelligence. The stories she shares, her own and of her friends, are both heartbreaking and yet full of hope as they tell the truth about the messages the church sends to women. The book serves as testimony that women, although often silenced and degraded in the church, are no longer willing to simply resign themselves to such injustices. Telling the truth, however painful, shines a light into the dark places illuminating what needs to change and *Unladylike* shines that light through its stories of countless women's experiences.

With its explorations of history and biblical reflection, *Unladylike* is a needed reminder of the ways the church has gotten off-track in regard to women as well as a heart-felt call for it to change its ways.

Julie Clawson, former pastor, mother, and author of *Everyday Justice: The Global Impact of Our Daily Choices*

***

This book demolishes the stain glass window enshrining Christianized patriarchy. It challenges the faulty logic and vapid theology used to oppress females and deny them their God-given humanity and their equal inheritance in Christ. Lend your voice, your influence, and get behind theseideas!

Mimi Haddad, President of Christians for Biblical Equality

***

Pam is a committed egalitarian with a complementarian past. *Unladylike* is the story of her journey. Whichever side you embrace, or even if you consider yourself somewhere in between, her story is a one woman-wrecking crew against sexism in the Church. Complementarians and egalitarians know sexism has no place in the kingdom of God. No matter what side you are on, *Unladlylike* is going to challenge you because Pam boldly guides us on a tour through the deeply rooted sexism in the evangelical sub-culture. But in the end, she guides us to Jesus, who was and who is and who will be the Liberator from all sexism.

Dan J. Brennan, author of *Sacred Unions, Sacred Passions: Engaging the Mystery of Friendship Between Men and Women*

***

Through heart-rending stories and compelling analysis, Pam Hogeweide examines the confusing messages American Christians are taught about women and their place in the church. *Unladylike* challenges us to move beyond complacent acceptance of inequality and exposes this discrimination for what it is -- *injustice* that followers of Christ must actively resist.

Emily Rice, community activist and writer

***

Unladylike: Resisting the Injustice of Inequality in the Church is the book that many of us have been waited to be written! Pam Hogeweide writes with passion, intellect, and clarity and challenges us to deeply consider how we are directly or subtly perpetuating gender injustice as men and as women in the body of Christ. This material is not about pointing fingers or shaking fists. Rather, Pam bravely inspires both sexes to actively create the change we want to see. With a powerful mix of biblical wisdom, cultural research, and real life stories, *Unladylike* will shake readers out of complacency to be active participants in gender equality not only in the church but in any of the systems we are part of. As a pastor and leader in the church for many years, I have seen the ravages of inequality and how difficult it is to change these deeply grooved patterns of injustice. I have also seen what can happen when men and women rise up and bravely participate in change. *Unladylike* inspires us to be part of setting ourselves and others--and the church-- free.

Kathy Escobar, M.A., Co-Pastor of The Refuge Church and author of *Down We Go: Living into the Wild Ways of Jesus*

***

For many Christian women today, an active involvement in social justice is the only avenue available by which we may work through our collective apology for having both the misfortune to be born female, and the audacity to find the traditional roles the Church has asked us to submit to somewhat less than satisfying. Pam Hogeweide is one of those pesky Christian females who insists that social justice must be first practiced by the Church before it can preach on the subject outside of it. In *Unladylike*, Pam clearly identifies and calls for a change to the inequities which still exist for women in an institution that has been for too long satisfied to accept women's sacrifices for its sake, but remains unwilling to make any of its own for theirs. If *Unladlylike* heralds a movement towards gender equality in the church, then count me in.

Jo Hilder, Blogger and contributing writer for *Burnside Writers Collective*

***

In *Unladylike*, Pam Hogeweide leaves no question about where her loyalties lie. Without a hint of prevarication and not appearing the least bit subtle, she draws her battle lines declaring, "The equality of women in the kingdom of God is not a side issue. I am not a side issue. The unequal treatment of women in the church is an issue of injustice." Pam goes to work dismantling long held assumptions, challenging misguided beliefs and exposing patriarchal power struggles. *Unladylike* is a powerfully written account of the equality Pam hopes for in this generation.

Dr Jim Henderson, Author of *The Resignation of Eve: What if Adam's Rib is No Longer Willing to be the Church's Backbone*

***

I applaud Pam Hogeweide. It took incredible backbone to write a book about the heart of this matter and to propel us toward imagining a better way. *Unladylike* is neither a figment of the imagination nor wishful thinking. It's about the injustice of inequality in the Church… as I read this book a song from my childhood kept throbbing through my head– "The buses are a' coming."

Bill Dahl Author of, *The Porpoise Diving Life – Reality for the Rest of Us: Picking Up Where Purpose-Driven Peters Out*

I was gravely warned by some of my female acquaintances
that no woman could expect to be regarded as a lady
after she had written a book.

Lydia M. Child, a 19th century women's rights activist
and abolitionist

Contents

This book is dedicated to the many unladylike women in my life.
You have helped me
become the woman I am today and I thank you.

Foreword

"**W**hy do we need another book on equality for women in the Church? Hasn't it all been said? What about good people who just see it differently?" These questions are a sample of what I hear in my travels throughout the land of Christendom in North America. My answer, "Until women are included in full equality in Christian churches across this land there is always a need for another voice, another story, another call to action and another theological argument."

My adult life has been spent serving churches that held a theological framework of biblical equality. I have been encouraged to pursue my desire to serve God according to my gifts and talents. As a single woman, I was part of a church planting team with two married couples. In 1995, I was ordained as the associate pastor of the church I helped plant.

Today, my husband Rich and I are the co-senior pastors of Vineyard Community Church in Shoreline, Washington. In addition, I am an Area Pastor Care Leader that brings pastoral care to seven churches in Vineyard USA's Northwest Region. At the time of this writing I serve as an Adjunct Professor at The Seattle School of Theology and Psychology in Seattle, Washington where I teach on Leadership to graduate students. Within the church, area churches and graduate school that I serve, I am completely free to be who God has made me to be. However, sometimes outside of these contexts, I often find myself among folks, both men and women, who resonate theologically with "soft patriarchy" or complementarianism. During those encounters, I often find myself feeling defensive for who God has created me to be, knowing there are those that believe I am somehow out of God's order.

Over the years I have read as much scholarly work addressing all sides of this conflict as I could. I want to be faithful to God. I am convinced that biblical equality is found throughout the biblical text when read through the lens of the Kingdom of God. From the beginning of our story to the end, we see God's intention that men and women are to be image bearers, working together to serve God as equal partners within creation.

Conflict in the church is not new. From the New Testament letters and all throughout church history we have seen good people disagree over serious issues. Issues such as the nature of Christ in the first century to slavery in our not too distant past, have caused great conflict between God loving people. Such is the continuing case with the debate over equality for women in the church. There are good people on both sides of this struggling for truth. As my husband says, "I wasn't a bad person when I held a complementarian view, I was just wrong."

Today as I sit in my home office writing this foreword, I am keenly aware of the young Reformed movement that has a growing influence in my city and across the nation. This movement validates and reinforces the oppression of women for a new generation. Through their theological view of male and female roles, this movement perpetuates the injustices against women in the church. Any denomination, movement or local church that excludes women from full equality with men, perpetuates a wrong the gospel of Jesus has made right.

In *Unladylike: Resisting the Injustice of Inequality in the Church,* Pam Hogeweide has taken the charge to name the injustice of inequality in the church through her own personal journey, stories of the many women she has encountered on her journey in real life and through writings. Pam draws on the scholarly works of those that have done their work in the original languages and historical context in which the biblical story comes to us and uses that work to undergird theologically the call—no, the plea—to not see this issue as a matter that falls into "disputable matters" (*adiaphora*), but rather see it as the justice issue it is. She quite rightly compares this issue at this time in history with abolitionist and social movements of the past with examples from slavery, the Women's Right to Vote Movement and the Civil Rights Movement. Pam calls us to action and to not give way to resignation:

In other words, those who are oppressed—even if that oppression is polite—must themselves find a new narrative for their lives that honors the full image of God they carry. This means that resistance is necessary, whatever that may look like in a woman's life. It means that resignation will get us nowhere. A sense of resignation that things are the way things are keeps women immobile and unimaginative."

I have heard Pam close-up and from a distance use her God-given talents to courageously speak out and take action. She is blazing a trail for women to fiercely take up arms and fight with the weapons of reading, praying, acting and speaking until thousands upon thousands of women are freed to take their place at the table. Pam powerfully gives us all the reason we need to stand up and be seen and heard in this fight for equality. My hope is that every person seeking to be faithful to the biblical text will read through this courageous work of naming "Injustice" and find their way to action. I commend Pam for her penning such a timely book on this most important issue facing the Church at the dawn of the twenty-first century.

Dr. Rose Madrid-Swetman,
Co-Pastor, Vineyard Community Church
Shoreline, WA
January 2011

Introduction

At times I wonder if I have allowed the passion of my convictions
to become dull. Have I lost my spunk in order to be a nice Christian
woman? I fear that I may have become too well mannered to do
much harm against the injustices in this world.

From my blog, *How God Messed Up My Religion*

I've been a writer for nearly a decade. Like most writers, I dreamed of the
day when I would write my first book. Trouble was, I could never settle
on what to write about. I'd kick ideas around until I kicked the life out of
them.

Through a series of personal events, I found myself blogging more
frequently about the inequality of women in the contemporary church.
I soon realized a pattern: comments would spike up as people tossed
opinions and Bible verses around in support or rejection of my egalitarian
views. The issue of women and equal treatment in the church was clearly
a hot button topic with passions running high from all sides.

It finally gelled for me. I knew I had enough fire in my bones to commit
to writing about the injustice of inequality of women in the church. But
the writing process has not been easy. It's been demanding and revealing. I
did not realize how much my identity had been affected by attitudes in the
church toward women until I began in earnest writing this book. The more
I researched and wrote, the more I uncovered forgotten scars and scrapes
in my life as a woman of faith.

Women around the globe bear marks of mistreatment from their culture. It is a man's world. But Christian women also bear marks from being devalued and dismissed within the world of church. Throughout Christendom, women are disallowed from certain positions that are reserved for men alone. Women typically are blocked from being in any manner of leadership over a man, even within marriage where the husband is deemed the final authority by default of gender.

Add to this that these issues are defended theologically as being God's will for women. And add to that the difficulty many women have resisting these inequalities as they are often shrouded with religious language.

Even when women of faith do possess clarity of their unequal status, there is often an attitude of patient waiting, as if praying and hoping for the best will make this injustice of inequality go away. Or that men will eventually see the light and tear down the *No Women Allowed* signs and raise our status from sidekick to partner.

In writing this book, I've discovered that freedom is acquired by conquest, not by gift.[1] Women must discover our personhood and our God-given voice and power for ourselves. A good Christian woman must be willing to be unladylike to defy the forces of inequality that have held her back.

It has been an uphill journey of decisions in which trails of thought to write about for this book. I quickly discovered the truth of the saying, "The more you learn the less you know." It is my highest hope that I have made wise decisions in the thoughts I followed and wrote about.

One of the decisions I had to make right away was how to speak of God. I am acutely aware that God is neither male nor female, yet we use language that gives God gender. God is most commonly referred to with male pronouns. Many other words associated with God and Christianity also favor male language such as kingdom, Lord, and Father. It is a dilemma to know how to address God.

In her book, *She Who Is*, theologian Elizabeth A. Johnson writes about this:

> What is the right way to speak about God in the face of
> women's newly cherished human dignity and equality?
> This is a crucial theological question. What is at stake
> is the truth about God, inseparable from the situation of
> human beings, and the identity and mission of the faith
> community itself.[2]

I agree with Elizabeth. How we speak about the gender of God is a crucial theological question.

For the sake of writing clearly, I have opted to use male pronouns in reference to God, which is also my practice when I speak of him. I am not assigning gender to God, but in the limitation of language, it is the means by which I speak and write of him. Consider this my disclaimer.

Another decision I had to make was in the telling of women's experiences and also my own. I have used real names in many of the stories, but in some instances, details have been changed to protect privacy.

A final note, this is not a theology book in the traditional sense, but it contains theology. I have attempted to offer a primer to several theological concepts concerning women and equality. I consulted with theologians I know to confirm accuracy, but as with everything I write, I bear full responsibility for any discrepancies that may have been overlooked.

I hope this first book of mine will resonate strongly with you. I hope it stirs something inside of you as it has with me. I hope you'll be inspired to be unladylike against the injustice of inequality that women of faith everywhere endure to this day.

Pam Hogeweide
December 2011
Portland, Oregon

PART ONE

INJUSTICE

The most common way people give up their power

is by thinking they don't have any.

Alice Walker, Novelist and Poet

Chapter One: A Polite Oppression

The injustice of Christianized sexism

> When a system of oppression has become institutionalized it is unnecessary for individuals to be oppressive.[3]

Florynce Kennedy, Civil Rights activist and feminist

My whole world of being a compliant female Christian was turned upside down when an unexpected person spoke into my life: a woman pastor. She was a demure woman, unassuming and down to earth. She had a casual authority about her in her posture and presence. There was warmth about her that was instantly engaging. I liked her right away. Her name was Rose Swetman. I had no idea that before the day was over, she'd say something that would rock my world inside and out.

I met her in Seattle during a small Christian conference that was being hosted by her church which she co-pastored with her husband. At first I thought they were a typical husband/wife pastoral team with the husband as the lead pastor and his wife as an assistant pastor. It didn't take long to sort out that Rose was the lead pastor, not her husband.

For starters, she did most of the talking. In public. From the platform. The only time I heard women talk in church settings was if the mic was handed to them. But here was a woman who was the one in charge of the mic.

Rose had been scheduled to speak along with a string of other speakers for the conference, but due to things falling behind, someone had to lose their spot. Being the gracious host of the event, she canceled herself. I was disappointed since I really wanted to hear what she was going to say.

At the break I caught up with her and asked what topic had she planned to speak on. "I was going to talk about the issue of equality between men and women in the church," said Rose in a matter-of-fact tone. A dozen women within earshot swarmed around us when they heard this.

Seeing the interest of the small crowd of women I asked Rose if she had time to share with us the things she had intended to say. We were all on a short lunch break, why not now? She readily agreed.

"So many women hit the stained glass ceiling of misogyny and end up resigning themselves to being the silent partner in church and even marriage," she began. The other women nodded in agreement, and I nodded, too, but anxiety began to tighten across my chest.

I kept listening as she talked about the need for mutuality in leadership and marriage. Rose said the subjugation of women to men in the church was nothing more than a replica of the patriarchal structures found in systems all around the world. "The church is supposed to be different. The church is supposed to be a place of freedom," she said. "Complementarianism[1] is not freedom".

Patriarchy? Misogyny? Complementarianism? I believed that women could teach and preach, but I never thought of it as such a big issue. Some churches believe in women teaching, others don't. As far I was concerned, it was a matter of Bible interpretation. There are so many doctrines that have multiple perspectives. I figured the topic of women was just one more issue that Christians debated about.

---

1   Complementarianism is a viewpoint based on an interpretation of the Bible that men and women are equal, but different in role. Thus, women cannot be pastors or Sunday morning preachers because it is not their God-ordained function.

More women spoke up with stories about inequality and sermons they'd heard. "The church I used to go to didn't let women preach or become elders because they said those roles were for men only," said one woman. A low murmur of empathy rumbled through the group, which now resembled a flash mob as we huddled together with Rose.

I remained quiet. I usually have plenty to say in a group discussion, but I had never heard women talk like this about equality in the church with so much conviction. I had always felt that it was a divisive topic and decided a long time ago that my beliefs about women and equality had to be tempered with diplomacy.

Every church up to that point in my life did not allow women to be elders or pastors. I never made a fuss about it. I figured there would always be something I didn't agree with so I needed to compromise and remain open to differing points of view. Besides, there are many things in the Bible that are interpreted across a wide spectrum of beliefs. It always seemed best to keep the peace and stay balanced and focused on the essentials. Women pastors, I thought, are a non-essential.

So it was a bit perplexing to hear Rose and the other women speak boldly about their thoughts and experiences with inequality. I was a silent observer, listening to everything, but I had nothing to say. My convictions about women and men in the church were neutral. I could not relate to these outspoken women who made the status of women in the church a much bigger deal than I ever had. I felt the contrast of my temperance with their passion. It made me uncomfortable.

I wondered if they all belonged to churches that were open to women being equal with men. Were they members of Rose's church? *Did they even go to church?*

"The problem as I see it with gender inequality is that it robs us of our personhood, for both men and women," continued Rose. "It puts us in preconceived roles of what a man's role should be and what a woman's role should be. That doesn't give us any room for what God has created us to be. God has led me to pastor. For someone to tell me that it isn't the right thing robs me and it robs the body of Christ."

I was mesmerized. My views about women in the church had shifted during my journey as a Christ follower, but I had maintained a tactful stance on the subject. I agreed with everything I was hearing, but her passion was making me uneasy.

"Gifting is Spirit based, not gender based," she continued. "If power is held only by males in the evangelical church, then we're missing out on half of what God has to say."

What she said next startled me. Words have power and what I heard next would have a powerful and lasting effect on my life.

"The issue of women and leadership in the church is not an issue of theology. It is an issue of justice."

This declaration came through loud and clear. My heart burned with prophetic energy. I didn't betray anything on the outside. I kept a straight poker face looking attentive while she continued to speak. But in the hidden part of me, the light had come on. I didn't realize it in that moment, but it was my awakening in seeing the true issue of inequality against women in the world of church: it is an issue of justice.

The issue of women being able to preach, teach, lead, and speak could no longer be confined to a neutral zone of doctrinal position in my mind. My heart was heavy even as my mind was electrified. Her words heralded something inside of me.

The issue of women and leadership in the church is not an issue of theology, but an issue of justice.

I had never considered it as a justice issue. I thought it was just a Bible thing, a matter of perspective. I never felt it was something to get upset about. Brothers and sisters should live at peace with one another. It means we have to agree to disagree, right?

I practiced this as part of my creed as a Christ follower, but it changed that day, in that handful of words spoken by a woman pastor. Everything changed, including me.

The equality of women in the kingdom of God is not a side issue. I am not a side issue. The unequal treatment of women in the church is an issue of injustice. Rose was right.

~~

Rose's words began an unraveling inside of me. My diplomatic Christian self was being loosened from a false ideal. All because of one sentence Pastor Rose had said. Those words became a tipping point in my history as a Christian woman. My thinking was being transformed as I reconsidered everything I thought of about women in the church in this new light.

I reexamined my code of remaining neutral about women teaching, preaching and leading. I had been sincere in wanting to maintain unity, which is good, but how does one excuse injustice in the name of Christian unity?

I recalled the many times I had remained silent while remarks, rules and rhetoric against women had been spoken in church settings, always by people I respected as leaders and Bible teachers. I just made room for it in my life. No fussing, no resistance. The second-class ranking of women in church was a standard I'd come to accept.

Like the time my husband and I attended a membership orientation for a church we had become active in. Topics discussed included the history of the church and what they believed which was a standard, mainstream Christian creed. At the end of the long presentation the pastor asked if anyone had any questions. I searched my mind for something overlooked. I am always the woman who finds something to raise her hand about. Then, it hit me. There had been no mention about women.

"What is this church's position about women and leadership?" I asked out of curiosity.

The pastor, a large burly man with a fatherly way about him, smiled and answered with a bit of preach in his voice. "We love women at this church. Some of my favorite preachers are women. At this church we let women preach and teach from our pulpit. We don't hold women back around here."

Then, with a sudden rush in his voice, the pastor slipped a "but" into the middle of his tribute towards women. "But you won't see women as elders or pastors. That's not taught in the Bible and we honor the Bible around here."

I nodded my head in courteous agreement. I had hoped this church had no barriers to women, but I was willing to let it go. He had his "but" and I had mine. At least they let women preach here, I told myself. All of the other churches I had ever known had not allowed that much. Women typically were not allowed to preach or give announcements or even lead worship. I surmised that this church was at least a little freer.

The room full of people seemed fine that, too. No one challenged him or asked a clarifying question or got up and left. That included me. It was unthinkable for me to let something like this keep me from fellowshipping in a church. It did not even come up while my husband and I drove home and discussed our thoughts about the membership meeting.

I viewed the notion of Christian equality between men and women as a private affair, a belief that had plenty of room for a wide range of perspectives. I didn't see it as an issue of injustice. Since I had no ambition to preach or be a pastor, I developed an attitude of compliance with the idea of women being restricted from certain roles in the church. I was resigned to acceptance as surely as I lived with the unending drizzle from the gray skies of my home in Portland.

When I did think about it, I'd tell myself that Christian women have it quite good. We don't wear burkas, right? I did not want to be petty about something doctrinal like women and leadership. Sometimes I thought the body of Christ was losing out on dismissing women from the pulpit, but I wasn't willing to fight for it. I found religious debates tiring.

A few years ago I mentioned to a woman at church that I wished we'd see women teaching from the pulpit. She gave me a funny look and asked, "What do you mean? You don't think women can be pastors, do you?"

A flutter of panic flew up in my mind. I didn't know her that well, but her intent gaze suggested that her Bible radar had been flagged. So I back peddled, committed to keeping myself out of a Bible controversy. "Well, I'm not sure about that," I said, "I'm not willing to say that I am one hundred percent convinced that women can be pastors, but I do think women ought to be able to use their gift of teaching for the benefit of all."

Her scrunched-up furrowed brow relaxed and she visibly leaned back out of my personal bubble, as she lost the scent of my unbiblical support of women in the pulpit. I was not willing to leave my safe middle-of-the-road position when I couldn't see the gain in doing so. I even felt good that I had managed to divert the conversation from a potential Bible feud.

As I reexamined that memory in light of justice I was beginning to realize that I wasn't being neutral at all. My lack of conviction had been an accomplice to the unequal treatment of women. My diplomacy was misguided. In my quest to maintain peace and unity, I had become a woman with a divided mind and heart.

It was during this phase of my spiritual journey that I stumbled into the impromptu women's listening party with Rose. What she said became a catalyst of change for me.

The issue of women in the church is not an issue of theology but an issue of justice.

Rose's words stayed with me long after the conference. I reflected for days and weeks on the implications of what she said, what did it mean for women and the church. What did it mean for me?

More flashbacks began to surface of instances where I had felt the tension of Christianized sexism. At one church, I was a volunteer in the youth group. I loved this faith community and felt a deep sense of belonging. At one of our staff meetings the youth pastor raised a concern that a parent of one of our teens had brought to him. "She's worried that we are allowing women to exercise spiritual authority over men when we allow our women and our teen girls to teach Bible studies. I told her not to worry, for that won't happen here. We honor the Bible in our youth group."

I felt conflicted. I respected this leader. Though our church was conservative and women couldn't teach up front on Sundays or be on the elder board, youth group had always been freer and women did sometimes teach Bible studies to mixed groups of men and women. Even I had taught. So what did this mean? Was he making a new policy about women teaching? Should I speak up on behalf of our budding female Bible teachers?

It was conflicting. I wanted to challenge him about it, but I talked myself into letting it go. "It's my problem. Just let it go. There's no need to make a big deal out of this." I sat there and kept my mouth shut for the rest of the meeting.

At that point of my journey, I didn't really have a theology about me as a woman in the narrative of the kingdom of God. This lack of theology about women and ministry kept me in an irresolute state of mind. I couldn't get riled up about inequity between men and women in the church if I didn't have a clear picture of what that meant. So for the longest time I accepted that it was inevitable for a church to not allow women to preach or pastor.

I reevaluated these old memories after hearing Rose's prophetic words. Seeing the treatment of women in the church through the lens of justice changed how I viewed these past experiences. I was beginning to recognize that what I thought was diplomatic neutrality was something else entirely: I had been complicit in the back rowing of women in the church.

The Ghost of Jesus vexed me as it became clearer that the issue of women in the church was not an issue of theology, but an issue of justice. This idea came like a gust of wind, ripping my code of diplomacy right out of my hands. A sense of regret flooded me as the implication of the kind of woman neutrality had made me. It was hard to realize that I had been an unwitting participant in perpetuating discrimination by my tacit silence. But it was even harder to think about churches I loved as being institutions that perpetuated injustice towards women.

I felt it was too harsh to judge churches as perpetrators of injustice towards women just because women are relegated to subservient roles. What true harm could that really be causing? This polite Christianized oppression of women looks innocent. It wears pretty clothes and invites you in for tea in a parlor filled with niceties and kindness. Before you know it, two thousand years passes by and here we are today, shackled by diplomacy and ladylike propriety with cold cups of tea.

It's been an awakening for me as a woman of faith. I no longer view the unequal treatment of women as innocuous. Seeing the true colors of injustice in how women are ranked lower than men in church has deactivated my code of diplomatic silence. I can no longer acquiescent with the hope that we'll all just get along. A woman denied her voice and place among her brothers is something I'm no longer willing to endure with ladylike acceptance.

Silence does not serve unity; it preserves the injustice of inequality.

Martin Luther King said, "Our lives begin to end the day we become silent about things that matter." That's what I had to learn, that women matter. That equality matters. That a woman's voice and full acceptance alongside her brothers matters. That oppression, no matter how Christianized and polite it may appear, matters. The issue of justice matters.

My life as a woman of faith began anew when I realized what Rose said was true. The issue of how women are politely oppressed in the church is not an issue of theology but is indeed an issue of justice.

Chapter Two: The Trouble with Being a Girl

The oppression of being female

> Every woman should be filled with shame by the thought that she is a
> woman ... the consciousness of their own nature must evoke feelings
> of shame.

St. Clement of Alexandria

> It is often easier to become outraged by injustice half a world away
> than by oppression and discrimination half a block from home.

Carl Rowen, Journalist

"Look, do you see them? Can you see the girls?" asked my friend Joni
as our motorcycle taxi, called a *tuk-tuk,* crawled along the crowded dusty
road. "See how young they are?" We were in Phnom Penh, the capitol city
of Cambodia, touring a Vietnamese slum neighborhood after dark to see
the nightlife. The bumpy road we traveled on was lined with brightly lit
open-air cafés. A fluorescent aura spilled out as we snaked our way along
the unpaved street. Horns beeped and pedestrians shouted greetings to
one another that created an atmosphere of revelry and merriment. But the
party-like energy of the makeshift boulevard was a façade that concealed
tragedy and human evil simmering underneath.

Joni Wise[4] had lived in Southeast Asia for thirty years. Originally from Kansas, she moved to Cambodia from Viet Nam to continue her ministry among migrant Vietnamese families who make up the largest minority in Cambodia. The two countries border one another and share a tense history that goes back hundreds of years. I first met Joni back in the early nineties when we both were living in Hong Kong as Christian workers in the Vietnamese refugee camps. She taught pre-school and I taught English. Joni and I lost touch many years ago, but had recently reconnected.

Although she now lived in the States, Joni made regular trips to Cambodia to provide guidance to her small network of staff and to bring much needed resources like money, books, clothes and ministry materials. She invited me to accompany her on one such trip. I was thrilled, having wanted to visit Cambodia since I was a young woman, but I was also nervous. Going to Cambodia would not be a tourist trip. I would be on a missionary tour with Joni as my guide. She would be showing me places rife with extreme poverty and sex slavery. I was walking into darkness.

"It's tragic what happens to these girls," said Joni as our tuk-tuk slowly crawled through the mayhem. I scanned the swarms of people, mostly Vietnamese men, to get a glimpse of the girls she had been telling me about. Joni wanted me to see for myself the atrocity of adolescent Vietnamese girls sold into prostitution. The poverty of their families is so severe that most girls who end up working in a "café" (*gentlemen's club*) were put there by their parents, though some girls willingly seek out this kind of work for the money.

Being born a girl in certain parts of the world is dangerous. Joni showed that to me as she gave me a tour of communities where oppression of the worst kind flourishes virtually unchallenged. The culture has absorbed it. It is normal. The oppression of their daughters is a part of life.

This kind of oppression is remote for most Western women. It is the stuff of documentaries and global ministries like what my friend Joni is doing. Many of us support abolition organizations that are working for the sake of the oppressed and some of us will travel to the far ends of the earth to help in whatever way we can. Churches send money and host campaigns for the sake of these oppressed women. We all want to help end human trafficking.

Yet within many of these same churches, women are oppressed. It's an irony that can't be ignored. It might not be human trafficking, but when a woman anywhere is suppressed from exhibiting her power or voice simply because she is female, this too, is injustice. It's not hard to find examples.

A few years ago I met a woman who felt certain that she was called to be a church pastor, but her denomination did not allow women to be ordained. She was forced to face the agonizing dilemma of deciding to leave the faith tribe she had known and loved her whole life, or to stay put and stifle her dreams with fatalistic acceptance.

At a conference one year I met a woman who had soared through seminary at the top of her class. "I was the only woman, and come graduation day, every single student had a pastorate lined up. Except me," she said. She was forced to look for opportunities as a woman pastor outside of her denomination.

A young woman I know is a gifted worship leader. Her skill was well known in her former church, but she was not permitted to lead during service. When she asked why not, she was told, "You'd be a distraction."

My friend Denie began to minister to the homeless in her town. Her fellowship group told her it wasn't proper for a woman to do this on her own. Someone in the group even challenged her character and motives for branching out into ministry to homeless men as a single woman. Denie resolved to stay on course, but decided to leave her fellowship group.

It is safe to say that none of these women would have experienced these kinds of obstacles had they been male instead of female. And yet these acts of inequity against women in the church are common and widespread. The culture of the church has made oppression so normal that it blurs into the scenery.

I do not think, however, that men are the problem; it is a pervasive patriarchal system in the church that is the problem. Therein lays the paradox: many in the church argue that affirming women as equals to teach and preach and lead freely as men is to conform to pressure from society. "I want to be sure I'm understanding the Bible and not conforming to culture," said one pastor who confided to me that he was exploring women's equality. And yet the roots of patriarchy, or male dominance in the church can trace its roots all the way back to the social codes of the ancient world, especially Greek culture. It is not kingdom of God Bible culture.

In the best-selling book, *Half the Sky: Turning Oppression into Opportunity for Women Worldwide*, Pulitzer Prize winning authors, Nicholas Kristof and Sheryl WuDunn, write in the introduction of their book that the moral challenge of the 19th century was slavery, but for this era they write, "We believe that in this century the paramount moral challenge will be the struggle for gender equality in the developing world."[5]

I think we can include the church in this struggle for the justice of equality between women and men.

~~

In her classic book on feminine adolescence, *Reviving Ophelia*, psychologist and author, Mary Pipher, notes that by junior high girls sense a lack of power in their lives, but they can't quite voice what it is that they are feeling. "Girls come of age in a misogynistic culture in which men have most political and economic power. Girls read a history of Western civilization that is essentially a record of men's lives ... as girls study Western civilization, they become increasingly aware that history is the history of men. History is His Story, the story of *Man*-kind."[6] There is incredibly powerful conditioning going on when a girl hears of the conquests of men. She sees male presidents and congressmen on television being lauded for their accomplishments, as well as the heroic tales of manly men.

A thousand small messages linked together create a cage of sorts: a caged worldview that trains the girl's mind to understand that power is the realm of males, and females are here to serve that power. It is rampant in the systems of government and institutions throughout the world. And it is rampant in the world of church, the place where the kingdom of God is meant to be the most liberating structure of all. Jesus said the Spirit of the Lord was upon him to proclaim release to the captives and set free those who are oppressed (Luke 4:18). This is the mandate from the Founder of our faith. Women have a long, long history of being oppressed within the culture they are born into. The church is meant to be counter-cultural in how we treat each other, including women. We are born again into a new culture, the culture of the kingdom of God which is a kingdom of love and justice. Christ following women need the world's message unraveled not affirmed, when we join the ranks of the church.

My friend Kim felt stirred by the Spirit to step into more roles of leadership in her church, and though her heart was nudging her, Kim's mind protested. She didn't have a worldview of women leading and speaking freely in public spaces. Culture taught her that women remain in the background. The church reinforced it.

While at a prayer retreat, she saw within herself a misogynistic filter through which she viewed women as well as herself. She experienced a tremendous awakening and shift in her thinking. Kim began to heal from the hurts of a lifetime of conditioning that women are less than.

Writer Sue Monk Kidd in her spiritual memoir, *The Dance of the Dissident Daughter*, describes this process as the "healing of the feminine wound,"[7] the culmination of cultural, social and religious formation that trains girls to become women who deny their power and voice.

Kim's acceptance of being less than in power and voice was informed by the conditioning she received in her formative years. She's quick to point out that she arrived to the church with her feminine wound. Church was not the culprit, her culture was. But once within the society of Christ followers, Kim's dysfunctional view of women, and of herself, continued unchallenged.

It is an unfortunate reality that women receive messages from pulpits that reinforce what culture has already told us about ourselves. It is not meant to be this way. The church is meant to be a refuge of justice and liberty in a world that is bulging with unjust systems of every kind.

Thankfully, when Kim and her husband moved to a new neighborhood they joined a Quaker church, a denomination that has esteemed women as equal with men for generations. It was within the sanctuary of her new faith tribe that Kim's feminine wound surfaced and she experienced not only an awakening to her value as a woman, but also healing from her growing up years when her girlhood was battered.

Her story is not unique. It is the same story for many women around the West as well as much of the world: men own power and women are to respect that power and serve it coffee and sandwiches like the good helpers we were created to be. The world taught us this. Sadly, our faith communities only confirm it.

~~

In her book, *Nice Girls Don't Change the World*, Lynne Hybels describes her journey of becoming an authentic woman and agent of change by embracing God's will instead of the perceived will of others for her life. She writes:

> Whereas a girl of any age lives out the script she learned as a child—a script too often grounded in powerlessness—a woman acknowledges and accepts her power to change, and grow, and be a force for good in the world. Whereas a nice girl tends to live according to the will of others, a good woman has only one goal: to discern and live out the will of God.[8]

I like that. It reminds me of the famous quote I have seen on t-shirts and bumper stickers:

Well-behaved women rarely change history.[9]

My friend Kim is a good example of this. She didn't become a rowdy rebel rouser after her awakening, but she did become a woman who was free to fulfill the call of God on her life. Cultural and religious walls that had blocked her vision had come crumbling down.

Kim's willingness to abandon her former ideals about women and herself brought her to a place of willingness to lead in ways that she could not consider in her former self-concept. She and her husband, together with their two daughters, moved to China to be teachers. It was during these years overseas that Kim's influence as a woman leader grew and flourished. She began to live in confidence that she had a powerful voice that was meant to be heard and used for good. Kim pursued opportunities to teach others about the ways of Jesus. She influenced many Chinese women to pursue their God-breathed gifts, since she now knew that the Spirit will empower who the Spirit will and it has nothing to do with girl parts or boy parts.

One summer Kim and her family came home to Portland for a short break. After dinner one evening she and I left my boisterous household of noisy children for a power walk, which for me means trying to keep up with Kim who tends to walk fast as if she's late for an appointment. We headed down a busy boulevard in my north Portland neighborhood. The Oregon sky blazed a blue canopy above us.

"Have I told you about my friend Ruby?" she asked as I pumped my legs faster to keep up with her stride. "No," I said trying gallantly to disguise my breathlessness from the power walk, "Who is she? A new friend?"

"Ruby is a Chinese Christian we met in our city," said Kim, her strawberry red ponytail bobbing up and down as we walked. "I wanna tell you about her. She's one of the most amazing women I've met in China."

Kim told me how Ruby was born into a family that didn't want her. They wanted a son and neglected her from the start, often leaving her outside in the alley to cry and squall as outcast children will do. That's how she got her name, Red Face. When she later took on an English name she adopted Ruby, a fitting as well as beautiful translation.

When Ruby was in her teens she left home for the big city to live on her own. What she really wanted was to go to university but in China, a nation of more than a billion souls, university spots are limited, and poor girls from small villages have little chance of securing a prized studentship. But Ruby contacted a university anyway. They told her she could not enroll as a student, but she could audit classes if there was a space for her in the back, and that she must not participate in any way. Ruby jumped on it. And this is how the red-faced China girl learned English as well as other things as an invisible scholar in the back of university classrooms.

Meanwhile Ruby had gotten a lowly job as a trash collector, truly one of the lowliest jobs a woman can get in a country like China. She was up early in the morning before the city woke up, prowling for trash pick-ups and chasing the rats that got in her way. After work she would go to school where she remained invisible while she silently attended classes like a hungry ghost in search of belonging.

About this time someone came along and told Ruby that there was a God, a Divine Creator who had breathed her into existence. She was not an accident. Ruby was meant to be born and born female. No matter what her family or culture told her, the liberating love of Jesus filled her bruised soul. Her life was not without meaning.

Ruby became a Christian and flourished in her new faith, somehow even obtaining a Bible, which can be difficult in communist China. Ruby began to read it and soon invited others to her small hovel of rented living space to read and study the Bible with her. People, including men, began to come on a regular basis and many of them were finding faith and hope in Jesus as Ruby led the way in Bible readings.

"Ruby started a church," continued Kim as we by now had reached the end of the pathway and had turned around to head back home. "She was a woman and there was nobody there to tell her that women aren't supposed to be pastors or start churches. She just did what God put on her heart without even thinking about it."

Kim and her husband became good friends with Ruby. Kim spent time with her on a regular basis, listening to her struggles and offering guidance as best she could. Kim became an influence in Ruby's life, encouraging her in the gift of her leadership, which was clearly a strength in her life.

Kim and Ruby were both given new eyes to see their own dignity. Culture no longer dictated who they were as women of God. Kim's discovery of the full personhood of women helped her mentor Ruby.

"You are like a pastor," I said to Kim as we were nearly home from our walk. "You know that, don't you? You are shepherding Ruby as she shepherds others. That's what pastors do. They shepherd."

"I guess so," said Kim, "The way her life is right now is amazing considering how her family treated her. And it was because she was born a girl. Just for being born a girl…" Kim's voice trailed off. We walked in silence for the next block. I was familiar with the Asian penchant for sons. Many cultures the world over prefer sons to daughters, but China has the special distinction of being a country where baby girls are discarded like city trash.[10] Ruby the trash collector. The irony was not lost on me. It is no wonder that female suicide in China is the highest in the world[11].

"Pray for Ruby," said Kim as we finally arrived back home, the sound of our daughters laughter spilling out of the open windows. "She still has a hard life ahead of her."

~~

I thought for the longest time that the injustice of the inequality of women in the church was my own hypersensitivity. But it's a word that describes a reality that exists for many women in their faith tribe. Oppression in the church is not an imaginary monster under the bed.

Oppression is the unjust use of authority. It's when a society's influence is used to tear down rather than build up. Oppression is a pastor telling his membership class that women cannot be elders or pastors in h church; it is the conditioning of women to be submissive to the men in their lives and deny their own power. It is the message that God sanctions the subjugation of females by divine design.

I do not like oppression. It strips a person of their dignity. Whether its race, sexual orientation or gender, discrimination against another human being because of their identity is unjust.

Because of human beings desire for power and control over others, oppression has been with us since the beginning of time. It is always necessary for those who are downtrodden to challenge the oppressive systems they find themselves in.

At different points in the history of America, citizens have become outraged at various forms of oppression that went unchallenged for generations. The women's suffrage movement in the early 1900's is one example. This group fought for women's right to vote.

The movie, *Iron Jaw Angels* chronicles the story of this battle for a woman's right to vote. In one scene depicting the resistance of Washington D.C. politicians, a voice-over says, "The female mind is inferior to the male mind. It would constitute a political danger." In another scene, activists stand outside the White House holding a banner that asks, "Mr. President, how long must women wait for liberty?"

This activism reached fever pitch when America entered World War One to help protect democracy in Europe. The women continued their protest to the president in front of the White House only this time their banners read, "He can't fight for democracy abroad and deny it here."

Another example of calling out oppression was America's shameful era of slavery. Less than two hundred years ago it was socially acceptable and entirely legal for a human being to own another in the United States. Slavery went unchecked during the infancy of America. But somewhere along the way enough people realized that slavery was an oppression that had to be undone.

We've gotten it wrong before. It is long overdue to see that we have it wrong again, that women are meant to have as much voice and power as men do. Gender does not disqualify, especially among followers of Christ. The church is meant to champion the oppressed, not join in with the culture in devaluing half the population because of gender.

For women of faith, it is a complicated dilemma to buck up against the injustice of inequality in the church when we recognize it.

When my kids were young my family was a part of a lovely, conservative church. Many families like ours made up the bulk of this fellowship. It was in many ways a typical American church with good people trying to love God and their neighbor in ways that honored the Bible.

When my baby son had to go into the hospital, the church women brought meals to my family. The pastors surrounded him and prayed for him. It was truly a caring and loving faith community

Yet discrimination flourished. There were no women on the leadership team. I once heard one of the pastors explain that women would not be allowed to exercise spiritual authority over men for that would "be against the Bible." The same pastor had shown compassion for my family and me when my son had been hospitalized.

I often felt a trace of irritation when I was reminded of what a woman's place in the church was supposed to look like. But I remained compliant (at least until Rose Swetman came into my life!). My acquiescence was a combination of diplomacy and ignorance. I was determined to censor myself for the sake of unity, and I honestly did not see it as inequality. I thought of the church's subservient view of women as a doctrinal matter. If you would have asked me then if I thought I was oppressed, I would have answered with a resounding No. But I also let it go because of my respect for the pastor. I liked him, trusted him and held him in high esteem. I could not remain offended with him or any of the other leaders in this church. They were men whom I trusted. Who was I to let women's equality become a divisive issue? There were too many things I did like in this church to allow the issue of women to get in the way. I never would have characterized it as oppressive.

This is why women like me have endured the inequality of our gender decade after decade in our communities of faith. I did not consider the treatment of my gender as oppression. It was just a nuisance, an irritant that had to be tolerated in order to preserve unity. When Bible passages such as the infamous "women be silent" passage of 1 Corinthians 14:34 were taught, I took it in stride. Discrimination? Oppression? I didn't think so.

The same church that taught me how Jesus saved me from my sins, was the same church that taught me that women must submit to the authority that God endowed men with. The same church that appealed to me to give to missions to help the oppressed on the other side of the world was the same church that taught that women are more prone to spiritual deception because of the sin of Eve.

Polite oppression has been the culture of every church I have ever been a part of (except for The Bridge which I'll tell about later). But oppression is still oppression, whether subtle or overt or passive or aggressive. Even within the church. Christianized sexism is oppressive to women. It ought not be this way.

The Bible teaches that the church is meant to be the body of Christ, his representative to the nations of the earth. We are to behave and live in the spirit of love and justice that Jesus demonstrated; how he elevated the status of the marginalized wherever he went, especially of women. The way churches treat women does not match how Jesus treated women.

Chapter Three: Second-class Citizenship

Equal but different does not equal justice

> I ask for no favors for my sex. I surrender no claim to equality. All I
> ask our brethren is that they will take their feet from our necks and
> permit us to stand upright on the ground which God designed us to
> occupy.

Sarah Grimke, 19th century abolitionist and feminist

When I was changing my mind about women and leadership after that revelation I received from Rose Swetman, I began to think long and hard on the biblical defense of the inequity of women. "Separate, but equal," I remembered one woman saying at a women's Bible study. "God made us equal, but we are separate in our roles. God created men to lead and women to serve. It's the natural created order." This is a popular view of men and women in many churches today. This explains why it is such a hot button topic. When believers are convinced that the will of God is for women to stay compartmentalized, any defiance towards it is considered deviant and unbiblical.

Labels like feminist or liberal get tossed around like scarlet letters to mark certain thought trails that must be avoided. I remember feeling a rise of embarrassment when a pastor's wife warned me about becoming an "evangelical feminist" when I questioned the idea of womanly submission. "You have to honor what Scripture teaches," she admonished.

"Don't get caught up in the culture war of women's lib." But I did get caught up, especially after the pivotal conversation with Rose Swetman. She highlighted for me the heart of the matter, which is that the issue of women in the church is not an issue of theology but an issue of justice.

Inequity, I finally realized, is indefensible.

The way Christ followers manage to defend the inequity and oppression of women is to call it something else. This is how I learned about the "separate but equal" argument, which has been around a long time. It is a common view among many Christians and gives us an out in how to reconcile the fair nature of a just God with biblical views that smack of inequality. It is the idea that God has made everyone equal, but there are different roles we are to fulfill in his created order.

For example, there are verses in the New Testament that seem to indicate the endorsement of the Almighty to subjugate human beings to slavery:

> Slaves, be obedient to those who are your masters according to the flesh, with fear and trembling, in the sincerity of your heart, as to Christ. (Ephesians 6:5)
> Masters, grant to your slaves justice and fairness, knowing that you too have a Master in heaven. (Colossians 4:1)

In today's America, we decry slavery and human trafficking. We blush with embarrassment and guilt that our ancestors practiced the horror of human beings buying and selling one another.

But according to many in the American church of the past, slavery was not only lawful but was even defended as the legitimate will of God. In fact, churchgoers and church leaders alike owned slaves … but not without controversy. The church in America during the 19th century was divided over its interpretation of scripture and slavery. Several denominations became fractured as churches became divided. At a general assembly for the Dutch Reformed denomination, debate ensued whether or not to admit churches into their fellowship if members were slaveholders. One pastor tried in vain to persuade the assembly to permit it arguing that slave ownership is not a sin. He bolstered his position with scripture passages that exhort slaves to obey their masters.[12] He was not a fringe lunatic, but representative of a theological point of view.

In his book, *A History of Christianity*, author Paul Johnson writes that the South Carolina Baptist Association produced a biblical defense of slavery in 1822. "There were standard biblical texts on Negro inferiority, patriarchal and Mosaic acceptance of servitude, and of course St Paul on obedience to masters,"[13] writes Johnson.

Slave-holding Christians hurled biblical texts (like the ones cited above) at their abolitionist brothers and sisters. If God did not will slavery, they surmised, then why did the apostle Paul provide moral guidelines for slave owners? Johnson highlighted the fact that 25,000 Methodist church members collectively owned more than 200,000 slaves in 1843.[14]

Abolitionists of the time were accused of being agitators and resisting the word of God. One preacher in Tennessee asserted that Christian abolitionists had "turned away from the word, in despondency; and are seeking, somewhere, an abolition Bible ... and an abolition God."[15] The same preacher also maintained that the relation of master and slave as being "sanctioned by the Bible," and compared it to the relationships shared between husbands and wives and parents and children.[16]

While many Christians were trying in vain to negotiate unity with one another, there were others who decried any religious defense of slavery. In a speech given in London to a packed out chapel, ex-slave Frederick Douglas gave a fiery indictment to Americans who practiced both slavery and Christianity:

> The church and the slave prison stand next to each other, the groans and cries of the heartbroken slave are often drowned in the pious devotion of his religious master... We have men sold to build churches, women sold to support missionaries, and babies sold to buy Bibles and communion services for churches.[17]

American culture and government also participated in defending the second-class citizenship assigned to people of color. In a civil rights case in the late 1800's, a black man was arrested when he attempted to sit in a whites only railroad car. A local judge ruled against the defendant and when challenged, the United States Supreme Court upheld it. The justification? Separate but equal accommodations did not stamp the colored race with a badge of inferiority.[18]

Why belabor this point?

Because there are strong parallels between the injustice of inequality our black brothers and sisters have suffered and those of women. Both groups of people have been told that God's plan for them is to exist in roles of subjugation and to accept their "separate but equal" status.

The same logic applied to the Bible to defend slavery is the same logic applied today to keep women of faith subservient. As I researched the history of the church during the Civil War, I was stunned with how people of faith could create a theology of oppression to keep the shackles of slavery intact. I was stunned even more as I recognized a pattern of theological reasoning that is used today to keep women in their place. I'm not the only one.

In the brilliant book, *How I Changed My Mind about Women in Leadership*, leading evangelical thinkers, pastors and theologians offer their personal stories of how they abandoned the complementarian view of women. Several of them write of how they saw the same parallel of biblical defense of slavery and the equality of women.

One contributor to the book, Cornelius Plantinga Jr., who is the president of Calvin Theological Seminary, writes how he changed from a limiting view of women to one of full equality. And it stemmed from his studies of slavery, specifically the defense of it from Bible quoting Christians. Plantinga writes that he wanted equality for women, but felt compelled to be faithful to Scripture. How could he reconcile the two?

> But then, that snowy afternoon in 1970, it hit me with the force of a revelation that the female subordination

texts and the slave subordination texts were in the same hermeneutical boat. The texts were sometimes in the same book of the Bible or even in the same chapter. I wondered by what hermeneutic such Christians were able to finesse or relativize the slave subordination texts, while insisting on the enduring application of the female subordination texts that came from the same neighborhood in the Bible?[19]

When I read Plantiga's account and others like it, it confirmed that I was not reaching for extremes by comparing the biblical defense of slavery with the subjugation of women. Oppression in all of its forms still remains oppression. What makes it especially outrageous, though, is when oppression and injustice are defended as just and even the will of God.

Christians are followers of Jesus Christ, whom we believe to be God come to earth in the flesh. Jesus made the Invisible God visible; Jesus taught and lived by the law of love. Kingdom equality reaches past all human social structures including socioeconomic and gender. There is no black or white, American or Chinese, or male or female. We are all one and we are all equal.

~~

Devaluing personhood is oppressive and misrepresents the kingdom of God. But sincere women of faith have been taught otherwise beginning with the culture of our femaleness.

The new documentary, *Miss Representation*, vividly confronts the prevalence of sexist messaging in media about women. Actress and activist Jane Fonda participated in the film saying, "Media creates consciousness and if what gets put out there that creates our consciousness is determined by men, we're not going to make any progress." I wholeheartedly agree.

Messages from both the culture at large as well as the subcultures we weave in and out of, such as Christian culture, inform our perception about others as well as ourselves. But as Christ followers, we are mindful of the words of Jesus who said that though we are in the world, we are not of it (John 14:13-19). In other words, though we move and have our being in fallen systems of the world, our identity is rooted in a higher kingdom, the kingdom of God, which is a kingdom of love and justice.

Many of us are familiar with what Paul the Apostle wrote, "Do not be conformed to this world, but be transformed by the renewing of your mind," (Romans 12:2).   Some Christians fear that welcoming women to full leadership and positions of authority is to conform to the world's standard.

Like an old pastor friend of mine who said, "I'm willing to take another look at Scripture about women and leadership, but I am concerned that I might be bowing to cultural pressures." But he's not. In fact, he'd be doing the exact opposite. Jesus was counter-cultural. He did not treat women in the same manner as the culture he was in. He resisted the cultural pressures of patriarchy. Unfortunately, the church did not and now it has become so embedded in our theology that marginalizing women is barely resisted. Full equality for women is blocked by concern for biblical accuracy. This concern is valid, yet it is troubling when doctrine becomes a means to keep women on the sidelines. Cultures the world over sideline their women. The culture of church ought not to be one of them.

~~

The early church was born during an era of tremendous gender inequity. Women were viewed as property with little to no rights. It is well documented that the life of our ancient sisters was rife with injustice and oppression for the sin of being born female. The taproot of this inequity? In one word: patriarchy.

In the introduction of his book, *The Gender Knot*, sociologist Allan Johnson defines patriarchy as:

> A society is patriarchal to the degree that it promotes male privilege by being male dominated, male identified, and male centered. It is also organized around an obsession

with control and involves as one of its key aspects the oppression of women.[20]

Allan also writes that patriarchy is "a system of inequality organized around gender categories."[21] Everyday patriarchy occurs whenever a man's voice or influence is given preeminence over a woman's simply because he is a man. It's when a woman is barred from pastoral duties because she is a woman or is disallowed from public speaking because only men can crowd the platform.

Patriarchy is an oppressive system that has infiltrated the church since the beginning.

One of the radical things about Jesus is that he frequently acted and spoke in an anti-patriarchal way. Jesus treated women as human beings. Two examples are how he dialogued with the woman at the well and also the two sisters, Mary and Martha. He did not perpetuate the patriarchal ideals firmly established in the Roman and Jewish communities he lived in. Jesus was counter-cultural.

Last year I met a woman who has felt the bitter cold of the winds of patriarchy. She grew up in a strict religious home where the roles of men and women were rigid. During her youth she watched her mother strive to be a good, upright Christian woman who submitted to her husband and pastors. The leadership of their ultraconservative church kept a firm grip on decision making and being the voice for their faith community. Women always occupied subservient roles such as childcare and coffee making. Not because they were better at it, but because they were women. This woman described how she began to realize from an early age that women were not as important as men. "I heard my dad say many times, 'I have the final say.' My mom could give him input and her opinion, but in the end, he made the decisions because he was the man."

This patriarchy was also true at the family's church. "Men were like the bosses, they were the pastors and elders and deacons and they were the ones who led everything like Bible studies and prayer meetings. Women were always the assistants. I didn't understand why women didn't get to lead things, too."

What she is describing is a typical church scenario and a typical system of patriarchy that relegates women to second-class citizenship.

There are many Bible teachers and scholars who spend a tremendous amount of energy decrying any challenge to patriarchy. Patriarchy is seen as normal so that any departure from its boundaries is judged as deviant. It is a pair of glasses we don't even know we're wearing.

Johnson writes:

> To see the world through patriarchal eyes is to believe that women and men are profoundly different in their basic natures that hierarchy is the only alternative to chaos, and that men were made in the image of a masculine God with whom they enjoy a special relationship.[22]

A patriarchal filter distorts our vision of God and our understanding of the Scriptures. It is all many of us have known since we were born and especially born again.

The book, *Recovering Biblical Manhood and Womanhood: A Response to Evangelical Feminism*, edited by John Piper and Wayne Grudem, is a 500-page prime example of how some view the world and God through the lens of patriarchy, though perhaps unknowingly. One contributing writer had this to offer in his commentary about male headship:

> So, was Eve's Adam equal? Yes and no. She was his spiritual equal and, unlike the animals, "suitable for him." But she was not his equal in that she was his "helper" ... A man, just by virtue of his manhood, is called to lead for God. A woman, just by virtue of her womanhood, is called to help for God.[23]
>
> He (God) allowed Adam to define the woman, in keeping with Adam's headship. Adam's sovereign act not only arose out of his own sense of headship, it also made his headship clear to Eve. She found her own identity in

relation to the man as his equal and helper by the man's definition.[24]

The identity of Eve being rooted in her role as Adams's helper is interpreted this way because of patriarchy. This ancient cultural force is alive and well in the Christian church of the 21st century. To question it is to question the authority of Scripture and the will of God. It is to challenge the status quo of one's faith tribe. This is very difficult for many Christ following women and men.

Tragically, many women are treated like second-class citizens in the body of Christ as if God mandates it. It shows up subtly leaving many women wondering if they are just being overly sensitive. It can be confusing for a woman to discern, especially if she has been raised her whole life in a patriarchal version of Christianity. We are in a fog of ambiguity of whether or not we are equal. It is like the writer said: women are spiritually equal, but ... and then that is where we live, in the uncomfortable tension of "but."

Women trivialize the injustice of inequity against our gender. We do this for we are conditioned to do so. We are brought up within and apart from the church to be accommodating, to give preference to others at the expense of our own thoughts and desires.

It creates an internal struggle for women. We're not wrestling with our brothers for a turn at the pulpit. We wrestle ourselves and often surrender as we decide that the equality we long for is really not that important. It would be amazing to see Christ following women live in a new kind of tension resisting the cultural message (within and outside of the church) that woman is less than. The liberating power of the Gospel of Jesus counters the values of the world; the church has been duped. Women have always been meant to live out the full *imago Dei* of God alongside our brothers. Not behind.

~~

At a women's group I was a part of a few years back, pastor and theologian Deborah Loyd introduced us to the book, *Women and Desire: Beyond*

Wanting to be Wanted, written by Dr. Polly Young-Eisendrath. Each week we'd read a chapter and discuss the topic such as how women give a lot of energy into building an identity that serves the wants and desires of others. The obsession with beauty is an obvious example of this. (If everyone else were blind, would we really spend all that money on hair and make-up?)

Her chapter on spirituality especially caught my attention. Dr. Eisendrath writes that, "Women cannot thrive in any religious or spiritual environment in which they simply follow rules that were invented, at least in part, to keep men functioning as Subjects and women as Objects."[25] She perfectly describes the dilemma that many women struggle with in church halls across America and beyond. But why do women put up with this? Why do women, who know how to run households and organize carpools and how to earn an income while raising kids and a host of other commitments, how is it that these strong, capable women put up with being second-class citizens in their faith communities?

It's complex and complicated, I know, but one root cause I have discerned is because of shame. Shame is one of the strongest emotions and one of the most effective driving forces known to the human condition. Shame pushes us out and stifles us down. Shame is where things like addiction and co-dependency find their fuel. Silence and complicity are bred in shame.

I have had a lifelong relationship with shame that began the moment I was born, not because of my parents, but because I was born as a female human being. As young as four years old, I can recall an early memory of shame when an adult compared my looks to another little girl. Later in the classroom I would feel shame for outsmarting boys when I knew too many right answers. I learned to raise my hand less often. Or later as an adult when ever I've observed men get preferential treatment over me only because of my gender.

To be a female human is to know shame and for some of us, like Christian women, shame becomes a steady companion that whispers quiet but intimidating thoughts into our minds. Things like, "Who do you think you are?" or "What's wrong with you?" Shame is the growling black dog that challenges our identity from coming out of hiding.

In her brilliant work on shame and vulnerability, Dr. Brene Brown shares how some of her research participants have described shame:

Shame is feeling like an outsider—not belonging."[26]

"Shame is like a prison. But a prison that you deserve to be in because something's wrong with you."[27]

I can relate to these. Shame lied to me for so long about my desire to be a woman with a voice and influence. Just wanting to have my own voice produced misgivings and second-guessing within me. The voice of shame would growl me into silence. "You just want to speak because you want attention. Do you see any other women teaching? Stay with the kids and other women. That's where you're supposed to be, not with the men," snarled the black dog until I yielded my desire to be heard like a good 1 Timothy Christian woman ought to do. [28]

When I was in my early thirties I attended a Bible seminar that both men and women attended. The leader of the study explained that those who completed it would have opportunity to teach at home Bible studies. "Except for the women. It's good that you're learning to study the Bible, and you can teach in women's ministry, but it would not be biblical for women to have authority over men."

When he said that a heat of shame coiled up inside of me causing my chest to tighten. Of course I wanted to be a biblically sound woman, yet I felt that I was just as capable of teaching as every man in that room. The low-growl of the black dog of shame kept me in my place, though; I wanted to keep in good standing with my faith community. I wanted acceptance in this church. I wanted a place to belong.

Dr. Brown offers another definition on shame, one that I think perfectly captures the tenor of the black dog growl:

Shame is the intensely painful feeling of experience of believing we are flawed and therefore unworthy of acceptance and belonging. [29]

Acceptance. Belonging. These two human desires reveal why many of us accept the injustice of inequality in apparent docility. It is why patriarchy has continued to thrive in many pockets of Christendom virtually unchallenged. Women are shamed into thinking that remaining subservient is God's will. For a woman to challenge that idea is to challenge God.

A friend of mine was enrolled in a conservative seminary here in Portland. She was pursuing pastoral studies despite the firm complementarian leaning of the seminary. One day during class she asked the lecturing professor why he thought women couldn't be pastors.

"Because the Bible says so!" he replied with a paternalistic tone. My friend sunk down in her seat, seething with anger and shame. What was worse, though, she recounted, was how no one in the entire class had risen to her defense, though privately several of her classmates had indicated their support for her pastoral calling. "I cried when I drove home. It was raining and it was like God was crying with me," she remembers.

My friend was devalued in the very place that was meant to equip her. The professor publicly shamed her by not taking her reasonable question seriously. This is the treatment women receive on an ongoing basis. Sadly, it becomes how we even treat ourselves.

Women are meant to be free to serve and lead alongside men. Collaboration and mutuality in leadership and servanthood is the culture of the kingdom of God. I believe with all my heart and mind that the day men and women learn to reflect, shoulder to shoulder, the full *imago Dei* is the day the powers of hell will shudder.

Dr Brown writes, "When we experience shame we feel disconnected and desperate for belonging and recognition."[30] The very thing that contributes to a woman's shame is also what keeps her ever negotiating for acceptance. Shame is cunning, bewildering and powerful. Shame is why women put up with being devalued and dehumanized in the name of a loving God. The deep root of shame keeps us from paying attention to the real culprit of our demise and that is the message of inequity towards women in our communities of faith. It is a message we have internalized.

Chapter Four: Sex and Power

From temptress to helpmate: the injustice of being a woman

> Women should not be enlightened or educated in any way. They should, in fact, be segregated as they are the cause of hideous and involuntary erections in holy men.
>
> St. Augustine

> I was pissed that God was a man and that Jesus was a man. I hated that I wasn't a man. I hated my gender.
>
> Michelle Foster, ex-Catholic turned seminarian

I became a Christ follower at the tender age of 18 at a Calvary Chapel on Las Vegas Boulevard. I had a profound experience of encountering God in such a way that turned my life around from being a self-destructive druggie kind of girl, to being one of those annoying Bible-thumping-demon-stomping-Spirit-filled-born-again-Jesus-freaks. I changed from coming home staggering on God knows what, to hitting every Bible study within a ten mile-radius two to three times a week. I had become a Jesus junkie and life was grand and beautiful. I made many new friends, which was good since I had taken up with thieves and outlaws. Most of my experiences with men had been on the negative side, too.

Meeting Christian guys in my church gave me an entirely new perspective on the goodness that is possible when a man is not just trying to have sex with you. I felt a new sense of security around my brothers. I reveled in my new Christian culture that insisted men control their sexual appetites, and women not set off the lusty hormones by keeping the visual of our girl parts to a minimum. Modesty became a new way of thinking for me in my baby Christian days.

Becoming a Christ follower was a revolution for me. When I entered the matrix of the world of church I was a scarred, bruised up girl who'd been used and abused for the desires of men. I needed a place of safety and refuge to heal from my sexual and emotional wounds. My church became my oasis in the Vegas desert.

There were a number of adults that took me under their wing and lovingly helped steer me towards a Christ-centered life. One woman counseled me to stay away from boys for at least a year. "Focus on building your relationship with God before you start dating," she advised. It sounded good to me, and so I thrust myself into a new, sex-free reality where men were my brothers rather than sexual partners.

When the sermons from the pulpit came forth that women needed to dress modestly so as not to "stumble our brothers," I vowed in my heart never to become a temptress who'd cause one of our holy men to have naughty thoughts. Thus, my new evangelical fashion sense began. I threw out my form-fitting t-shirts in favor of tent shirts. I'm a curvy woman—always have been—but I learned to wear oversized shirts as if I was an insecure middle-school girl who didn't know what to do with her hips and boobs. So I hid them, under an evangelical burka of lust-stopping, flowy fabric.

I felt safe around the men in my new social circle. Light-hearted flirting occasionally lit up, but mostly I hung with a pure crew of monasticized men. And I loved it. I loved the rapport of conversing with guys and hearing their thoughts and insights without sexual tension muddying up the boundaries. It was all good. I relished being a part of a faith community that demanded sexual purity. I felt safe and for the most part, I was safe.

It was within this cocoon of newfound spirituality that I trusted the pastors to show me how to travel upon the Christian path. My life had been considerably impacted by my conversion to Christianity. I had been transformed from a young woman who just wanted to stay wasted all the time, to a new creation in Christ who was discovering the powerful and redeeming love of God. I was full of gratitude and wonderment that Jesus loved a floozy like me.

~~

The safety of my faith community brought me a life free of reckless sexuality. But over time, the message of modesty became burdensome, though I would not have been able to define it had you asked. The responsibility for keeping men from being tempted for a woman's fruits began to weave threads of shame into my feminine identity.

One Sunday, the pastor spoke from the pulpit saying that men had complained to him about women who showed up to church improperly dressed. "To be brutally, honest," he bellowed, "some of our women are dressed as if they were prostitutes!" His pronounced judgment took the air out of the auditorium. I forced myself to keep my eyes on him instead of looking down to see what I had worn that day. I dared not look at myself or at others. Tension mounted inside of my belly as I determined that I would never come to church looking like a hooker.

I was absorbing a new paradigm about human sexuality in my new Christian culture. One thing I was learning was that women possessed sexual powers that could ruin a man. From the very beginning with our mother Eve, women have had the burden of using our womanly ways to wreck good men. A woman's sexual power had to be disarmed lest she unleashed a torrent of ungodly desire in her brothers in Christ.

As a daughter of Eve, I'd inherited her stigma for bringing down the entire human race with sin. No wonder shame prevails with deep rootedness in women's collective identity. Feminine power is made to be the culprit for a man's sexual appetite. The prevailing culture continued to suggest it was my responsibility to keep his fire burning low. But for many of my Christian sisters, this is an unfair equation that reduces men to mere sexual beasts and women being sexualized to the point that our humanity becomes hijacked.

I often organize women's listening parties for Christian women. We come together and talk about how the church has informed and shaped our identity. Invariably we will end up discussing some aspect of sexuality before the evening is over. At one listening party, women began to swap memories of past experiences in church youth groups.

"We were going to church camp and fliers were handed out for the guys and a different one for the girls," said one young woman with a Pentecostal church background. "The dress code for girls was so long. No spaghetti straps, no two-piece swimsuits, no skirts or shorts above the knees, no form fitting t-shirts or blouses."

"Yes, but isn't that good?" chimed in another. "Don't teenage girls need guidance so they don't become a distraction for teenage boys?"

The room became lively with discussion as women debated the need for dress codes.

"What it did," she continued, "is teach me and every other girl that we can't trust guys and we can't trust our own bodies. We have to hide our curves."

It's a complex topic layered with cultural messages. On the one hand, we live in a sexualized culture where women are conditioned to flaunt their bodies for approval in a patriarchal society. A friend of mine who is a high school teacher laments the scanty outfits some of his female students arrive to class in. "They become a big distraction to the rest of the class." When visiting the high school my two teenagers attend, there are plenty of young women showing as much skin as they can get away with. Immodesty is clearly a cultural norm.

So I am sympathetic to youth groups that see a need to establish a dress code, especially for their young women. I used to be on church staff for youth many years ago. One night a 15-year old girl showed up to youth group with her top so low that we could see her bra. There is a tension, though, when young women of faith continually bump up against dress codes and wardrobe monitoring. Culture wants to sexualize us; church, it seems, wants to desexualize us. In the end, women are left staring in the mirror and wondering if our skirt is too short for Sunday service.

Jesus was counter-cultural in the context of the society he lived in as well as the religious culture he engaged with. Jesus did not shame the woman caught in adultery (what was *she* wearing?) and he freely associated with women of ill repute (what did *they* wear?). Jesus ignored the sexual objectification of his female friends. He treated women as human beings.

Writer and lay theologian Dorothy Sayers gave an address to a women's society in 1938 titled, *Are Women Human?* that has since been published in a book of the same name. She writes, "What is repugnant to every human being is to be reckoned always as a member of a class and not as an individual person."[31]

Gender identity is informed and shaped by culture and that includes Christian culture. When women are repeatedly given a list of do's and don'ts aimed at our feminine nature, it teaches women not to trust our bodies. Women then equate visible curves as visible sexuality, as if admitting one has boobs is admitting that one has sex. This is far from true, yet for women of faith, we are relegated to neutering ourselves in order to appear sexually pure and to keep our brothers from burning with lust.

At my women's listening parties, we often have passionate discussion about what it is to be embarrassed of our feminine nature. "I was taught to hide my girl parts," said one woman about her upbringing in the church. "Oh yeah, "agreed another, "my job as a Christian woman has been to desex myself in public as much as possible. It's a wonder I'm allowed to menstruate!"

"I felt like I wasn't allowed to be human," said another friend. "To be a woman is to be less than, to somehow be defective and incomplete."

"Women are considered temptations," said another. "I learned to stunt my sexuality while I was growing up in the church. I wore loose clothes and kept my hair short. Some people thought I was gay."

Women have sexual power, no doubt about it. But instead of developing a healthy sexual image, Christian women are instead conditioned that our sexuality hovers at the edge of lasciviousness. We can't be trusted around men. Our curves get in the way.

In his refreshing book, *Sacred Unions, Sacred Passions,*[32] author Dan Brennan says the reason for this is that we have only two narratives for determining relationships between men and women: one, the sexual romantic story and two, the danger story. He explains that men and women (in culture and in church) see each other through these two storylines. We're either looking for a hook-up (if we're single) or we're nervous about illicit relationships if women and men relate too closely. This deeply affects how women are treated in church and how men and women view one another.

I remember the message of woman as temptress becoming personal when I made an appointment with one of the pastors of my large church. I was 18-years old and a new Christian. This was my first ever appointment with a pastor and I was feeling nervous, as if I was going to the dentist. The pastor stood behind his desk and welcomed me to come in and sit down. I gently closed the door behind me as I would for any similar appointment. I had barely sat down when the pastor came from out behind his desk and to my bewilderment, opened the door a few inches. "Just to be safe," he said as he returned behind the fortress of his desk.

"Oh," I mumbled with a hint of blush rising to my cheeks. Was he concerned that I might jump his bones? Or that he'd jump mine? I wasn't sure, but I internalized a message that *women alone with men* meant trouble.

Not long after that incident I had a job interview at one of the hotels on the Strip. When I was called from the waiting room to enter the interviewer's office, he did not hesitate to shut the door for our appointment. I flashed back to the appointment with my pastor the previous week. It was confusing.

The sexualizing of women is nothing new. But I surmise that in a kingdom of equality such as the kingdom of God, women are to be realized as fully human and not reduced to our sexual parts. This is not to say that women (nor men) are to slather around as sexually charged exhibitionists. What I am saying is that women must not have our sexual nature held responsible for a man's sexual nature. This not only shames women, but it shames men. It creates an image of men as being unable (and unresponsible) for controlling themselves, that men cannot be trusted with women, nor women with men. This leads to the separation and isolating of the sexes from one another, for they cannot be left alone together. It's why the pastor has to leave the door open when women come to see him.

A church I was a part of a few years ago experienced a scandal. It was the familiar story of a church staffer becoming inappropriate with a young woman and then getting caught. He was a well-liked man in this community and his termination came as a great shock to most of the congregation.

I was close to the young woman involved and knew the whole story of his attempts at initiating a sexual relationship with her. Her identity, as well as most of the details, was kept discreet from the congregation. I was dismayed, though, when at a home Bible study that week members of the study began to hold the unknown woman responsible for his fall from grace.

"Women will tempt men. They come in and seduce them and wreck their ministry and marriage," said one man.

"We need to pray for his reputation to be restored," said another.

"It's spiritual warfare," said one woman. "I think I know who she is and I knew she was trouble the minute I met her."

I was astounded at the assumptions flying around the living room that night. But in hindsight, I can see how a young woman would be vilified to carry (yet again) the burden for her brother's sexual misconduct. When women are sexually objectified, we bear the brunt of the shame. This is not kingdom culture.

In the kingdom of God, we are to emulate the harmony of relationship between men and women without sexualizing it or demanding that women neuter themselves in order to relate to men safely.

Dan's book addresses the tension of male/female relationships in the church. My friend Kathy Escobar, who's a pastor of The Refuge in Colorado, posted an interview she had with Dan on her blog. He provides some insight about male/female relationships:

> Kathy: The whole topic of cross-gender friendships is very rarely talked about by many church systems. In fact, there is a great resistance to cross-gender mixing and much more emphasis placed on keeping the sexes segregated. Where do you think this resistance comes from?
>
> Dan: There is a great sexual fear between men and women. There are two stories about men and women in many church systems: the sexual romantic story and the danger story for all those who don't have romantic trajectory possibilities. There is a huge shame-based culture embedded in our sexuality where we segregate men and women into particular roles, relationships, and groups. When only these two stories are told, there is deep fear for men and women to be alone, unless they have a romantic path open. These stories profoundly shape the way communities view men and women. Even as communities recognize women as pastors/leaders, if these two stories are their most prominent communal narratives,

men and women will not experience the fullness of what
Jesus is calling us to. [33]

It is without a doubt a controversial subject. But I contend, as does Dan in his book, that men and women are not meant to be constrained by a puritanical code that insists the sexes remain segregated out of fear of sexual impropriety. Rather, we must allow love and healthy discretion guide us in our male/female relations.

In the comment section of the interview at Kathy's blog, Dan added,

> Yes, the dreaded danger story looms large with sexualization when it comes to possibilities of trust and meeting alone. In the romantic sexual story, of course, men and women are wired to want to have sex together if they meet alone, even if they weren't thinking about it moments ago. We all know this from romantic comedies, love stories, pop songs, and Joseph and Potiphar's wife. This is what happens all the time when only two large narratives shape our sexuality: the romantic and the danger.[34]

We need the narrative of God's love to guide us in male/female relationships. Not culture.

The sexualization of women fragments the image of God. Women then feel pressure to desex ourselves in order to collaborate with men. Sexualizing women kills the unity. It lends to the injustice of inequality against women. Where then is the whole image of God, the *imago Dei*, to be discovered in a complete picture of male/female integrated in sacred union?

~~

If dress codes and skirt lines are a hot topic, the concept of marital submission is a fiery inferno. In the world of Christian women, the dreaded S word stirs up tensions of subordination, marriage equality and biblical authority. Marriage is the perfect microcosm of how traditionalism in the church impacts the home. How male and female roles are carved out in a marriage partnership reveals our theology and beliefs about female subservience.

My husband Jerry and I once went in for some counseling as we were in need of a marital tune-up. One of the first questions the Christian counselor asked was, "What do you each believe about submission?"

Jerry and I were on the same page viewing marriage as a partnership of mutual submission. "It helps me to know what couples think before we proceed," explained the counselor.

The issue of submission essentially centers on gender. Complementarians hold that women are inherently designed to serve and assist, that submission is a biblical virtue for women of faith and that men are designed to lead, that by default of their maleness they are the designated head of household.

Grudem writes:

> "Be submissive to your husbands" means that a wife will willingly submit to her husband's authority and leadership in the marriage. It means making a choice to affirm her husband as leader even when she dissents. Of course, it is an attitude that goes much deeper than mere obedience, but the idea of willing obedience to a husband's authority is certainly part of this submission...[35]

Authority is core to this issue of submission, the idea that husbands possess God-breathed authority to rule the marriage as well as the home. One of the roots of this belief stems from the concept of headship. Most Christians have been taught or at least heard of the biblically held view of headship, particularly that of husbands over wives. It is based on a passage from Ephesians 5:22-24:

> Wives, be subject to your own husband, as to the Lord, for the husband is the head of the wife as Christ also is the head of the church, he himself being the Savior of the body.

From this verse many Christian women have been taught that deferring to their husbands as the ruler of the home and marriage is a biblical mandate. To obey your husband is to obey God. But is it? Did the Apostle Paul intend these verses to construct a template for all marriages through all of time?

I don't think so. After reading several books about this subject, I believe Paul is teaching a principle of marital love and respect in keeping with the cultural context he lived in. At the time of the Apostle Paul, women had little to no rights, especially wives. They were the property of their husbands, barely above a slave. J. Lee Grady writes about this:

> In New Testament times, a man's idea of "ruling the family' was to keep his wife (shut) away in the house to do back-breaking chores, tend the family farm, provide sexual gratification and bear as many children as he wanted so he could have plenty of laborers to harvest the crops. If she died in childbirth, he found another wife. If she didn't please him in bed, he paid a younger woman outside the home to meet his sexual needs. If his wife shamed him, he beat her. If she dared to run away, he found her and beat her again.[36]

In light of the cultural context, we can see that Paul was like Jesus. He was counter- cultural in his advocacy for women to be well treated. Paul was introducing the radical Christian concept that women are to be regarded as equals, that a husband is to love his wife as if loving his own body. This was a much different concept of marriage than the typical Jew or Roman was accustomed to at that time.

The headship controversy is also fueled by a verse from 1 Corinthians 11:3:

> But I want you to understand that Christ is the head of every man and the man is the head of a woman and God is the head of Christ.

The concept of headship hinges on the word head, which in Greek is *kephale*. What does *kephale* mean? There is debate about this word and what Paul intended when he penned these words nearly 2,000 years ago. Some Greek scholars believe *kephale* means "authority over" while others think it is used to convey the idea of "source or origin." [37]If scholars can't agree on what *kephale* means how else can one investigate this passage's meaning?

At first glance, it appears that the Apostle Paul is offering a hierarchal view that ranks women in the bottom: God ⇨Christ ⇨Man ⇨Woman. This is a traditional perspective that views the world through a hierarchal filter. But is this accurate? Wouldn't this mean that Paul is contradicting himself when he writes about equality in other passages?

> There is neither Jew nor Greek, there is neither slave nor
> free man, there is neither male nor female; for you are all
> one in Christ Jesus. Galatians 3:28

In the book, *Why Not Women?* Bible scholar David Hamilton does some detective work to decipher what this passage could mean and if it establishes the doctrine of headship. From his studies, Hamilton has determined that interpreting *kephale* to mean source/origin fits much better with the rest of Paul's writings. The passage can then be read this way:

> But I want you to understand that Christ is the source and
> origin of every man and the man is the source and origin
> of a woman and God is the source and origin of Christ.[38]

Hamilton explains that Paul was not providing a flow chart of hierarchy that headship is derived from, but instead was giving a timeline. The man and woman cited in this passage are Adam and Eve, so that the passage is meant to convey that Christ is the Creator of all, of man (Adam) and from Adam came woman (Eve), and later in time, Christ came from God. [39]

The unique burden for a Christian woman is that if she finds herself at odds with the teaching of headship/submission, she may presume to find herself at odds with God himself. For if she is defying the Scriptures by not submitting to her husband's authority, she is also defying her Creator.

I married my husband Jerry more than two decades ago. In the beginning, I tried to fulfill the traditional womanly role as a submissive wife. Jerry didn't communicate an expectation for this, but I stumbled my way through those early years of marriage trying my best to be a good, submissive wife as I was taught to be from the pulpit.

I respected my husband, yet it became clear that I had more of a public voice than he did. In gatherings, meetings, Bible studies, etc ... I was much more vocal than he was. In traditional roles, a man's leadership is exhibited in public spaces while a woman rules the home. Our marriage did not resemble a traditional complementarian model. Jerry is laid back and comfortable being in the background, while I'm the one who wants to participate in public discourse, whether in home Bible studies, speaking and teaching or blogging.

Instead of recognizing that we had different giftings, I internalized an image of Jerry and of myself as being flawed. Based on a traditional model, we were. It all stemmed from me believing that wives are meant to be submissive to their husbands. It was a phantom that haunted my marriage for more than a decade.

But Jerry never once used his "man card" in our marriage. He always wanted to work things out together in collaboration. It was me who struggled, for my identity as a woman had been so informed by church teaching on submission that it left me confused. Isn't he supposed to be more "leaderly" and I'm supposed to be more demure? I hid my embarrassment that our marriage did not match the evangelical ideal.

Traditional hallmarks of a husband's headship, such as leading in family devotions and mealtime prayers were absent from my home and marriage. Jerry is a very private man when it comes to his spirituality. He is very uncomfortable displaying his inner life. It sometimes caused tension for me, such as when others would come over for dinner. Who would pray?

I would nervously look over at my husband as guests would sit themselves around our table. It was always a fifty-fifty chance of whether or not Jerry would offer up a short and awkward prayer of thanks, or if he would instead turn to me and ask, "Why don't you pray tonight, Pam?"

I cannot know if the many different guests who have graced our table ever had an inkling of the headship/submission clash simmering beneath the surface. But I have an idea that at least one family did. They were our most conservative friends. As we all sat down together around my dining table, the moment of truth rushed upon me. I looked at my husband, a frozen smile on my face as I tried my best to cue him to pray. Jerry brushed his hand across his leg, a nervous gesture when he's stalling. Just as he drew in his breath to speak, the husband of the family broke in, "How about I'll pray?"

Jerry's tense posture relaxed, but I sat there with my fake, happy wife smile plastered across my face like cheap lipstick from the corner drugstore. A flutter of shame and embarrassment buzzed around my gut. There was no question who was the head of their family. Whenever we went to their home for dinner, there was no ambiguity about who would pray the blessing over the meal. I idealized about their marriage whenever I agonized over mine.

At times I envied his wife as she cooked and baked and stayed home full-time with their children. It was not even a question of whether or not she would work outside the home. He was the provider. She was the homemaker. It worked for them, and though it was never said out loud, there was a feeling of superiority, as if they were living out God's intention for the created order of men and women in superb synchronicity.

Over time, our relationship with the couple became more strained as we loosened up in our domestic roles. I discovered that our marriage worked, not as an evangelical traditional marriage, but in the partnership we had forged with one another. It was ok that I was the louder one in the marriage and Jerry the quieter half. I was letting go of submission and headship and in the letting go, my marriage breathed freer.

I had a dream a few years ago of Jerry and I showing up to a banquet. When we signed in, we were directed to different dining halls, one for men and a separate one for women. Not only that, but Jerry was given a shirt to wear that matched all the other men and I was given a pair of shoes that matched the other women.

We went to our different dining rooms, but soon after I sat down my feet began to hurt. The shoes didn't fit right. Nothing felt right. I finally left in search of Jerry only to find him in search of me. We peeled off the shoes and shirt we'd been given and dropped them in the garbage on our way out of the banquet hall. Once outside the building, we began laughing like high schoolers who had just played hooky.

Getting out from under the submission/headship teaching brought joyful liberty for me in my marriage. I no longer hold up my marriage against an ideal that it can never live up to. It's not who Jerry and I are.

I met a couple not too long ago. The wife is a strong leader of a thriving ministry. She is vivacious and instantly charms the room with her presence. Her husband is much different. He has a mild personality and is soft spoken. He does not play an integral role in her ministry, but instead helps hold the fort down at home. He also works full-time, but when it comes to leadership, his wife is a natural.

She is often swarmed at church by many who want to connect to her, while he takes care of picking up the kids from their Sunday school classes. In a headship/submission model, it looks like they both are failing in building a biblical marriage. And I feel for them, for I know that they are part of a faith community that tells its men to man up and its women to get out of the way. I hope they both know the joy of accepting one another and celebrating the unique union each marriage is. There is no cookie-cutter biblical model.

In the Bible, the Psalmist wrote that God desires truth in the innermost being and that in the hidden parts of a person he will make known wisdom (Psalm 51:6). Being true to who I am has been liberating in the most intimate relationship of my life.

Jerry and I are still committed to each other, more than twenty-three years later. Mutual acceptance and respect for each other's personhood has served us well. Jerry doesn't need to man up and I don't need to quiet down. We only need to honor the woman and man whom God has made us to be.

~~

Submission robs the woman's voice and allows her to abdicate her responsibility in the marriage. This can be easily seen in decision-making. Her husband may ask for her opinion, but for those marriages firmly entrenched in a submission model, a woman can remain unburdened by the responsibility while her husband bears the weight of it.

My friends Anne and Brad talked about this with me. "When I was single, I was looking for someone to marry who would be the head of the household," says Anne. "Someone who'd make the decisions. While I was dating Brad, I kept trying to figure out what he wanted." As their relationship grew more intimate and Anne pressed Brad for the ideal partner he was looking for, she became frustrated with his answers.

"I told her I'd be happy with whatever my wife would want to do. Work outside the home, go to school, stay at home, whatever she would want. But when I told her this, she burst into tears," says Brad. Anne was looking for someone to make decisions for her life. Instead, she got freedom.

They married and established a partnership of mutuality and collaboration. Eventually Anne and Brad became marriage enrichment leaders and lead an annual retreat for married couples. They have observed the hits marriages take when the submission model is applied.

"Women have frustrations that their men are not doing enough. All these expectations that men are supposed to do things that are maybe not even who they are," says Anne. "And some women are looking for someone else to make decisions about their life. Submission becomes an out in that everything in their life is their spouse's fault. Or they feel guilty that they need to pray more and submit better." This is a good description of my marriage in the early years. I wish I'd met Anne and Brad back then!

~~

At a recent women's listening party at my house, a newlywed told us that her evangelical roots from her childhood were beginning to affect her relationship. "I'm worried of emasculating him," she confessed as she processed out loud with the group of how to find her way in establishing a partnership with her new husband. The art of navigating disagreement and conflict is tricky for any new couple, but my heart went out to her. I was familiar with the constricting and confusing forces of patriarchal gender roles.

"Can I address that?" said Jodi, a new friend who I had met at a Christians for Biblical Equality conference the previous month. "Let me give you new language to use," she offered. "It's not about emasculating your man. Are his man parts still intact?" Laughter rippled around my living room. "Women do not emasculate men with our strength. But what we want to think about is, are we demeaning personhood? It's about personhood, not gender. It's not about emasculation," said Jodi. A murmur of agreement hummed around the room. That was it. Personhood.

Jodi was a good one to say it, too. I had invited her to share some of her story at my women's listening party. At the conference, we had spoke at length about her painful journey exiting her church of many years when she could no longer endure the injustice of inequity against women. She filled in more details at my listening party, starting with how she and her husband navigated the waters of husband/wife gender roles.

"My husband and I didn't agree with the hard line that the fall happened because of Adam," said Jodi. "We knew people who taught that Adam abdicated his authority when he allowed Eve to eat, and that this is why men must keep authority over their wives or bad things will happen."

I caught my friend Nancy's eye when Jodi said this. At the last listening party I held, Nancy had told us that when she was younger a church elder had advised her not to travel alone to a Bible conference while her husband was gone on a mission trip. "That's how Eve got into trouble when she got away from Adam," the churchman told her.

Jodi continued, "But we did assent to the idea that because of the created order, the man should be the head of the house and the leaders in the church. Through various circumstances I ended up being the primary breadwinner; unusual for our faith community as most women stayed home with their kids.

"I worked very hard to prove that I had a career *only because* it was delegated by my husband, but I also made sure I kept up the house and motherhood. My husband Dave was willing to help out. I was very successful in my career and eventually ended up as a corporate consultant, but I was not allowed to serve in comparable roles in the church or to ask questions about church business such as budgets and leadership decisions.

"One Sunday, I was asking one of our elders about the church budget as I had some concerns about certain line items and some decisions about how money was being spent. I was basically told that I was not an elder and was not qualified to be an elder because of my gender, and so I was not qualified to be asking the questions I was asking.

"The next day I was on a plane flying somewhere for my work with a CFO of a major company asking me, 'Jodi, explain these numbers to me, I don't understand what is going on here." I thought, 'What's wrong with this picture?'

"Over the years I knew something was wrong with the rigid view of men's and women's roles in our community, but I also avoided ever reading a book on the topic or exploring the topic intentionally and theologically. I talked about the issue from time to time and asked questions but never really committed it to prayer. I think I knew deep down I had a lot to lose by taking my egalitarian leanings any further. So, I confined myself to bitching about male headship in private while publically affirming it with my attempts to be a good wife and mother. I was seeking personal affirmation for my biblical obedience despite our unusual family structure.

"Unfortunately, it took a marital crisis for me to seek God's truth on my own. I began to question everything, including God's love for women. I cried out to God and wondered if women were just a supporting cast in

God's grand redemptive drama he was bringing to pass through the men. I determined to study God like the men and went to seminary to get my own answers.

"Within one semester I was able to build a biblically based argument for equality in the home and in the church. When shown the evidence, my husband assented to the idea intellectually, but when I announced that I was leaving our church, he balked. I told him I was going, but he could stay if he wanted. I could no longer deny the truth about God's Word and the truth about the strict hierarchical misogyny that plagued our community.

"Eventually, my husband decided to support my decision and left with me. When he shared our decision with our closest friends, he was met with a theological argument that ended with, 'So, you are just going to throw out 2,000 years of church history?'

"I can't understate the grief of leaving our community. I would be lying to say that I am so happy to be in an egalitarian seminary and church that it doesn't matter. It does matter and it hurts. But, being obedient is seldom easy and I have the deep peace of knowing that I am right where God wants me to be. And though there is grief, I am really enjoying the freedom to be me, the me God created and the me he wants to use for his glory and purposes."

Jodi wrapped up her riveting story telling us that her marriage is now rooted in equality rather than hierarchal roles of headship/submission. We were so touched by her journey that several women were in tears when she finished. Her story was our story of how powerful the church is in shaping our identities as women and as wives.

Many people, especially those outside of the Christian culture, might wonder, Why not just walk away? Many have walked away, like Jodi, and it is not easy. For most of us, it's complicated. So we avoid it. We choose to not wrangle with the inequality staring us in the face. It's a power struggle akin to David and Goliath, only many women feel utterly powerless to even show up to the battle.

We need to help each other revise our story if the one we find ourselves in is suffocating our identity. A subservient version of ourselves is inauthentic for many women, as it was for Jodi, for me and so many others I've talked with over the years. There are those women who are happily content with the submission/headship model, but for many women it is a corrosive force that threatens their identity and even their marriage.

If submission/headship diminishes us to a lesser version of ourselves, then we must search for truth until we find it, and when we do, it will likely cost us something.

Sue Monk Kidd writes, "The truth may set you free, but first it will shatter the safe, sweet way you live."[40] I think I hear Jodi giving a hearty amen to that.

Chapter Five: The Bible Tells Me So {Part One}

The Search for Biblical Equality

> The women are to keep silent in the churches; for they are not permitted to speak, but are to subject themselves, just as the Law also says.
>
> 1 Corinthians 14:34

> There is neither Jew nor Greek, there is neither slave nor free man, there is neither male nor female; for you are all one in Christ Jesus.
>
> Galatians 3:28

I've been involved in discussions and debates about the issue of gender equality in the church for more than twenty years. I've been on both sides of the issue, having once been a devout evangelical woman who was desperate to please God and gain and keep the approval of the men and women around me, whom I admired very much. Even ten years ago I did not feel as strongly as I do today about the equal status of women.

I have known women who have long felt the disproportion of equality between men and women in their faith communities. It eats away at their soul, slowly corroding their sense of worth and value in a religious culture that is meant to be their refuge of safety. Some women quietly leave, slipping out the backdoor without a word being said. They wander away from the haven of church determined to find an open meadow where being a woman is not a liability. I know women who've never come back, though their argument isn't with God; it's with the people of God who maintain an ideology of gender inequity and defend it in the name of Bible doctrine.

In the summer of 2011, research organization the Barna Group, released its latest findings in regards to American women and the Christian faith. The number of women attending church has declined by 11 percent according to their research. Church volunteerism has fallen by 9 percent, which is to be especially noted since women have long served behind-the-scenes to keep church programs humming along.[41]

Barna's study summarized "that the only religious behavior that increased among women in the last 20 years was becoming unchurched." We can speculate why women are disappearing from the pew (at a faster rate than men, says Barna) yet I have to wonder if part of it has to do with the misogyny that permeates the corridors of Christendom?

I like to believe that this shift of women leaving is positive, an indication of resistance to the injustice of inequality in the church. In fact, when I first read this study, I had just met three different women who left their churches (but not their faith) as a result of sexism they experienced in their faith communities.

I remember the first time I heard of a woman leaving her church over this issue. It was years ago. I was part of a thriving non-denominational church that was complementarian in belief. At the time, I agreed with complementarian view so it was a non-issue for me at my church.

The woman who abruptly left our fellowship was not much older than me. She had been quite involved as a volunteer so it was noticeable when she stopped showing up.

"Why did she leave?" I asked someone who was seemed to know what was going on.

"She wanted to teach."

She wanted to teach? Teach what? What did that have to do with her leaving?

Oh, not teach what. Teach to whom. She wanted to teach men.

Apparently, she had told one of our pastors that women ought to be allowed to teach at home Bible studies and from the pulpit like men do. When he told her it's not biblical for a woman to teach the Bible to men, she decided to leave. I was astonished. Why would that bother her so much? Why wasn't she content to teach women's Bible studies or children's ministries? There was more than enough opportunity to teach in these realms. She had been told this, but she decided she couldn't be in a church where women weren't allowed to teach as freely as men.

It's on her, we decided. She could have taught in women's ministry, but that wasn't good enough for her.

"She's in the wrong," said the church woman, "She better be careful, too, that she doesn't go too far off the track of biblical truth."

It's good that she left, I decided since she had this kind of disagreement with our church. And though I never consciously defined my feeling about her departure, and hardly anyone else even mentioned her leaving, there was within me an unsettled feeling, a sense of disquiet that she could go off the rails like that. It would be years after my changed mind about women and leadership before I reinterpreted her departure as an act of protest.

Whatever was going on her life, she clearly had two things: a love for the Bible and a love for equality. The church context we were in made this a field of tension for the two to co-exist. Obviously, she had tired of living in that tension. I'll likely never know more specifics about her story, but I have since come to know many women like her who cannot reconcile staying in a church where women are taught that the Bible esteems men more than women.

The Holy Scriptures are at the heart of the controversy over whether or not women can lead, teach, preach, prophesy or possess pastoral or spiritual authority (especially over men). Or more accurately, the *interpretation* of the Bible is at the heart. Two camps of biblical interpretation have created a clear line in the sand of position: Complementarians commonly hold that women and men are equal, just different in that men are inherently created for leadership roles and women inherently created for helper roles. Egalitarians believe that the Bible issues no limitations towards women who are free to lead, teach, preach, prophesy and possess pastoral authority (even over men).

For most Christ followers, understanding the Bible is the primary way of discovering what God's will is for human beings. How and what we are taught from the word of God informs us in our spiritual journey. And it informs us in how to regard male/female relationships and leadership models.

Although I am a committed egalitarian, I recognize my complementarian past. My views shifted over the years as I read up on multiple perspectives about women and spiritual authority. When I did begin embracing an egalitarian position, I considered it a theological position. For this reason, I was not willing to debate about it in order to avoid contention and division. Also, I felt that it was a trivial issue, a non-essential to what really matters and that is the Gospel message of God's love.

This was emphasized to me in a conversation a long while back with an acquaintance. We were talking about the issue of women and equality in the church, and I wondered out loud why the church we were in did not permit women to teach or exercise spiritual authority over men. It was a rare conversation as I usually remained private about my belief except with close friends. But this woman had invited me over for and we had been getting to know each other for quite some time.

"I love our church, the people are amazing, but I think it's wrong to keep women sidelined," I confided. She listened ever so graciously, but without a sympathetic word. Instead, she told me a story.

"A woman missionary held the position of leader at a missionary outpost due to the shortage of men. The conservative missionary society she belonged to normally frowned upon women leading, but with no men available, they were forced to make an exception.

Eventually, a man did come along and he immediately was installed as the leader of the missionary enclave. The veteran woman missionary stepped down and submitted to his leadership.

"But that's not fair," I protested. "Why did she have to step down to a rookie missionary just because he was a man? She's the one who's been there all those years and has all the experience."

My friend, who was quite traditional in her role as a wife and woman of faith, pursed her lips together and calmly folded her slender hands into her lap.

"She was happy to submit to his leadership since what really mattered was the need to stay focused on ministry. She was there to serve the people of the country she was in, not pick battles with men over leadership positions. And that's why she thinks Christian women need to let go of evangelical feminism. It's a distraction to what really matters, which is the building of the kingdom of God."

I sat there wordless, the logic of this appeal both shaming me and confounding me into silence. This was why I didn't like to bring it up. I felt selfish for being fixated on women's equality, as if I was in danger of dishonoring the body of Christ with my trivial concern.

Her story cornered me with the belief that the issue of women's equality and the church was petty. It was insignificant. Unimportant. What I would not realize until after that pivotal conversation with Rose Swetman, was that in relegating the issue of women as unimportant meant I was relegating a segment of humanity as unimportant. Women are human beings. I am a human being. Justice demands that oppression of any human being must cease. Women are not a distraction to the mission of the Gospel; women are both recipients and messengers of Jesus' message of liberty and grace.

Oppression is never trivial. How we view male and female roles are not trivial. Just ask the women who are leaving their churches because they can no longer ignore the disparity of equality. It was not trivial for them.

What does the Bible say and how is it being used to oppress women? I want to show you key passages that are typically cited to keep women relegated to the margins of their churches. How we view the Bible and how we interpret it is the linchpin of inequality against women in the name of God. The binds that tie us to a patriarchal view of ourselves has to be recognized before it can be unraveled.

~~

Words have power and none as much as the sacred text known as the Bible. Its words have provided comfort, hope and encouragement for millions down through the ages. The poetic imagery of the Psalms as well as the prophetic anguish of the Old Testament prophets inspires artists and theologians alike.

The Bible says of itself that it is sharper than a two-edged sword (Hebrews 4:12). Swords can be used to protect and defend. Or to attack and maim. It is no secret that many have used the words of the Bible as a weapon against others.

When Christians argue, we spar with Bible verses like sword-wielding pirates fighting over a treasure of gold. Christ followers are zealous for truth. The problem is we sometimes wound one another in our passion to persuade others to our point of view ... which we are convinced is the only right view.

Debates and theological throw downs are common in all corners of Christendom, much of it is healthy, but there are certain topics that rage fierce and deep. Women and equality would be one of them.

Even women who possess a devout faith in God and the scriptures struggle with the meaning of specific difficult Bible passages. Some challenge the authority of the Bible, finding it difficult to trust anything between its pages when the imagery of the book is male dominated with male heroes and a male deity.

And then there are those bothersome passages that smack of misogyny and give anti-Christian pundits plenty of wood to fuel their rhetoric fires.

What can a woman do with verses like 1 Timothy 2:12 where Paul writes that women ought not to teach men but remain quiet? Or what about 1 Corinthians 11 that says man is the head of woman? And let's not forget my all-time favorite verse that has been hammered into a Christian woman's consciousness like a second-graders multiplication table: Wives submit to your husbands (Ephesians 5:22). It's no wonder that many flee the confines of patriarchal Christendom that cage a woman's identity. These verses create havoc as many either defend or refute them with tremendous fervor.

It is an unfortunate reality that the words of the Bible have been oppressive towards women for centuries. The male-dominated language of the Bible and the all-male authorship of the sixty-six books that make up the biblical canon transmits the message that women's voices are not worthy to be heard within its pages. When God's Spirit inspired the Bible scribes to write holy words, apparently only men were eligible. The Bible appears to be a male-centric sacred book.

Sue Monk Kidd points out an article from *The Atlantic Monthly* that confronts this gender gap:

> The Bible is no stranger to patriarchy. It was written if not entirely by men. It was edited by men. It describes a succession of societies over a period of roughly 1200 years whose public life was dominated by men...It talks almost only about men. In the Hebrew Bible as a whole, only 111 of 1426 people who are given names are women. The proportion of women in the New Testament is about twice as great, but still leaves them a tiny minority. [42]

A stranger of the Bible reading this description might wonder how its women adherents are able to accept the Bible's authority in light of this portrait of inequality.

Then there are a handful of verses in the New Testament that are used to form an ideal of biblical womanhood from a traditional point of view. These passages woven together seem to create a version of a Christian woman with all the qualities reminiscent of a Stepford wife. The ideal biblical woman is so…ladylike.

She is quiet:

> The women are to keep silent in the churches, for they are not permitted to speak, but are to subject themselves, just as the Law also says. If they desire to learn anything, let them ask their own husbands at home; for it is improper for a woman to speak in church. (1 Corinthians 14:34-35)

She is submissive to male authority:

> But I want you to understand that Christ is the head of every man, and the man is the head of every woman, and God is the head of Christ…for man does not originate from woman, but woman from man; for indeed man was not created for woman's sake, but woman for the man's sake. (1 Corinthians 11:3,8-9)

> A woman must quietly receive instruction with entire submissiveness. But I do not allow a woman to teach or exercise authority over a man, but to remain quiet. For it was Adam who was first created, and then Eve. (1 Timothy 2:11-13)

She is a submissive wife:

> Wives, be subject to your husbands, as to the Lord, for the husband is the head of the wife as Christ is the head of the church, He Himself being the Savior of the body. But as the church is subject to Christ, so also the wives ought to be to their husbands in everything. (Ephesians 5:22-24)

> Wives, be subject to your husbands, as is fitting in the Lord. (Colossians 3:18)

> In the same way, you wives be submissive to your own husband so that even if any of them are disobedient to the word, they may be won without a word by the behavior of their wives. (1 Peter 3:1)

These are the passages that burden women with biblical idealism, but even worse, these are the verses used to sustain and defend Christian sexism. When Christ followers debate about having a woman preach or admitting a woman to the elder board, these are inevitably the verses that will be cited to keep her banned. Pulpits lack a woman's voice and presence because of these verses. Or rather, because of *the interpretation* of these verses.

For many years I accepted what I was told to believe about myself, as a woman, from the traditionalistic churches I belonged to. The women I fellowshipped with and served alongside rarely spoke up about the gender disparity around us. Men led. Women helped. That's the way it was since that's what the Bible taught us about ourselves. Or so we thought.

For instance, the idea of submission. Women and men throughout Christendom are taught that female subservience is a biblical virtue. Didn't the apostle Paul proclaim to the church in Corinth that "man is the head of every woman?" (1 Corinthians 11:3) And did not Paul also write that "women must quietly receive instruction with all submissiveness?" (1 Timothy 2:11)

Many Bible teachers have taught that these verses, and others like them, indicate that God has designated women to excel in helper roles and to refrain from leadership roles that would exert authority over men. It would be out of God's so-called created order.

John Piper explains:

> When the Bible teaches that men and women fulfill different roles in relation to each other, charging man with a unique leadership role, it bases this differentiation not on temporary cultural norms but on permanent facts of creation.[43]

Permanent facts of creation. Men in leadership roles, women in helper roles to men. Permanent.

As in **Permanent.**

This attitude, when conveyed as biblical truth, is daunting for many women to challenge, especially if we are unaware or unwilling to explore outside of the traditional stream of thought.

Many years ago when I lived in Hong Kong, my friend Tracey challenged my traditional views about women. "Pam, you have to remember that the Bible was written by men for men. But God doesn't respect men over women. We are equal and are equal in gifting and calling," she said with a lilt from her British accent. "Women can, too, be pastors and priests and bishops and whatever else on God's earth the clergy want to call themselves. It's more biblical than you realize."

This conversation with Tracey sparked in me what my friend Deborah Loyd calls, "a spirit of inquiry." I began to investigate these teachings for myself. What I found began to unravel the curtain of patriarchy that had veiled my view of women and men. When I began to read and study about these verses, I discovered a wide-open vista of biblical equality. God's word, it turned out, was not so sexist after all.

One of the early books I read was by John Temple Bristow, *What Paul Really Said about Women: The Apostle's Liberating Views on Equality in Marriage, Leadership, and Love*. This book helped explain how Paul's writings have been misinterpreted through the lens of ancient attitudes towards women, most notably, Aristotle's influence.

The famed Greek philosopher had firm ideas about women. "The courage of a man is shown in commanding and of a woman in obeying,"[44] was just one of his many ideas about women. He also taught that men were to women what a soul is to the physical body, teaching that men are meant to rule women as the soul is meant to command the body.

Bristow reveals how Aristotle's philosophy would have influenced and even distorted the early church fathers understanding of male/female relationships:

> Aristotle thus laid a lasting philosophical foundation for
> the notion that females are inferior to males. He formalized
> the practice of sexual discrimination and offered learned

authority to the belief in sexual inequality. Centuries later,
church leaders who themselves were a product of Greek
culture and education interpreted Paul's writings from
the perspective of Aristotelian philosophy, even to the
point of assuming that when Paul wrote of the husband
being head of the wife, he was simply restating Aristotle's
analogy of the husband being to his wife like one's soul
to one's body. [45]

Aristotle's influence staggers me in how his voice is still heard these many
centuries later, though we mistaken it as a voice of divine authority.

I had never heard anyone teach this perspective in the many sermons I
had listened to up to that point in my Christian journey. Reading Bristow's
book was like taking a history class on the roots of my faith. I had never
before considered how cultural bias could influence traditional views of
scripture such as the subservience of women. The penny, as they say, had
begun to drop.

Bristow reviews several of Paul's hardest passages. For example,
he deciphers wifely submission from Paul's passage in Ephesians 5 by
looking at the ancient words stripped of cultural stereotypes of women.

"Wives, be subject to your husband," has long been interpreted to
mean that women are to submit to the authority of their husband by virtue
that husband's are male. But Bristow shows how the ancient language that
Paul wrote in actually does not communicate this. Instead, says Bristow,
Paul was introducing a model of marriage based on sexual equality.

"Subject," it turns out is a difficult word to interpret. Of
the different words available in Paul's time, he chose a
word that's meaning is closer to something like, "offering
support."[46]

Bristow explains the nuances of the original Greek and how it can be
inadequate at times in English translations. For "subject," he explains at
length the nuances of the Greek word *hupotassomai* that Paul chose when
he wrote the original passage:

> ... *Hupotassomai* cannot be translated simply "be subject
> to" without implying a subservient position. The phrase
> "be response to the needs of" expresses the essential
> meaning, but it is too long and unwieldy for a translation.
> "Serve" suggest the role of the servant to master, and
> "minister to" might imply some unspecified but inherent
> weakness among husbands. Perhaps the phrase "be
> supportive" is the most suitable among the choices offered
> by our language for a readable translation.[47]

To be supportive versus to be submissive has an ocean of difference between it for women in relationship to husbands, especially for our sisters from ancient times.

This is but one example of the many that Bristow unravels. I was astonished at how simple his logic was, yet bewildered that I had not been taught this before. I viewed this as critical information in helping to uncover the intended message of Bible writers. From cover to cover, his book helped open my eyes to the compelling evidence in the New Testament that esteems women.

Bristow ends his book affirming the apostle Paul as a champion of equality:

> Surely in the long history of Christian teachings regarding
> the relationship of women and men, the model that gained
> favor in the Church was not the one voiced by Paul, but
> by a pagan philosopher five centuries older, defended in
> the sanctuaries and cathedrals of the Christian faith by
> quoting the words of Paul, as translated, out of context,
> without reference to that ideal close to Paul's heart that
> he so earnestly sought for the church, that there be sexual
> equality among Christians—"neither male nor female, for
> you are all one in Christ Jesus."[48]

With Bristol's perspective, it's possible to defend Paul when others malign him as the root of misogyny in the church. His writings about women have been misrepresented and as a result, women have felt the brunt for centuries within the church of Christianized oppression.

The spirit of inquiry awakened within me would not rest. I continued to read many other books throughout the years about biblical equality including 10 *Lies the Church Tells Women*, by J. Lee Grady. In this neatly organized book, the author confronts how cultural bias and misinterpretation has drastically affected women throughout the body of Christ. I appreciate what he wrote in his conclusion:

> We are like the Pharisees, smug in our enlightened understanding of the scriptures. They were keepers of the law, but they became so entrenched in their own interpretations of the Bible that they didn't recognize the incarnate Word of God when He stood in their midst.
>
> When Jesus visited the temple on the Sabbath and healed a woman who had been bent over for eighteen years, they dismissed the miracle and indignantly accused Jesus of breaking the Sabbath (See Luke 13:10-17). These men were so locked into their religious traditions that they could not recognize the hand of God at work right in front of their eyes. And they quoted the Bible to defend their opposition to Him.
>
> We desperately need to be delivered from the spirit of the Pharisees. Countless women today, like the woman in Luke 13, have been healed by the Savior and are eager to tell multitudes about His love and power. Jesus did not tell the crippled woman to shut up, yet we insist on silencing women who are called to preach—and we are quick to quote scriptures out of context to justify our position. [49]

I like how Grady calls out the misuse of scripture against women. I had learned to accept the misuse of scripture in my early years as a Christian because that was all I knew. It is what I was taught. What is interesting to me now is how oppression was unchallenged in my life. I see now how I allowed myself to become conditioned by others who unknowingly guarded and defended a biblical viewpoint steeped in patriarchy. Together we perpetuated it. This is how the injustice of inequality is passed down as a legacy from one generation to the next.

Another tremendous book that has helped me absorb biblical equality is the more weighty scholarly work of *Discovering Biblical Equality: Complementarity without Hierarchy,* edited by Ronald W. Pierce, Rebecca Merrill Groothuis and Gordon Fee. This book is an outstanding collection of writings from evangelical scholars who confront biblically defended inequality head-on.

In one of the articles, *Equal in Being, Unequal in Role,* the writer challenges the common biblical teaching that gender destines a person to certain roles and prohibits from others. The writer uncovers how this belief lessens a woman's personhood:

> If I am equal in my human being, then I am equal in my female human being, because female is what my human being is. Or, conversely, human is what my female being is. At all times and in every respect, my "being" is essentially and intrinsically female and human. If I am unequal as a female human being, then I am unequal as a human being.[50]

I could not agree more. The view that God's created order destines women to subservient roles and yet attempts to insist that subservience and equality are compatible, is like trying to mix oil and water.

An old friend of mine sent me a Facebook message last year. She told me that she had stopped going to church out of frustration with the messaging that women are less then. Despite her incredible musical talent, she was disallowed from performing on the worship team because of her gender. Only men could possess lead roles on the team. She was welcome to play a supportive role, which she complied and tried to be content with for years. But the constant reminder, Sunday after Sunday, that women (although equal!) were barred from key worship positions, finally crushed her to the point of leaving her fellowship.

Her grievance was not about ambition. She was not vying for a star position in her faith community's worship ensemble. She just wanted fair treatment based on her talent, rather than unfair exclusion based on her gender.

When the injustice of inequality flourishes in a church, its women will suffocate.

The church sorely needs champions of equality. One champion I happened upon in recent years is the organization, Christians for Biblical Equality (CBE). The mission of CBE "affirms and promotes the biblical truth that all believers—without regard to gender, ethnicity or class—must exercise their God-given gifts with equal authority and equal responsibility in church, home and world."[51] I love what the header says at CBE's website:

Advancing a biblical foundation for gift-based rather than
gender-based ministry and service.

I had an opportunity to attend part of a conference CBE hosted in Seattle the summer of 2011. I was surprised at the diversity of people who were in attendance. I expected it to be predominantly Christians from more liberal denominations, but instead I met people from all kinds of backgrounds including conservative. There were also a remarkable number of men in attendance as well. But what really made an impression on me was how deftly biblical the presentations were from the array of more than qualified speakers.

For example, one of the main sessions was led by a New Testament theologian who spoke on, "*Justice and Equality for Women Created in God's Image: The Scriptural Mandate for Ministry and Marriage.*" Clearly this is an organization that is determined to provide relevant information to today's debate about women in the contemporary church.

CBE is not a feminist-agenda driven organization. They are a group of people highly dedicated to communicating biblical equality as effectively as possible. They offer a wide array of resources including their publication,

Priscilla Papers, an academic journal that provides scholarship concerning gender equality and justice issues. CBE is a great example that there is more than enough compelling biblical evidence for the mutuality of leadership and spiritual authority of women. It is not a fringe belief of a few liberal Christians who are "out there." Biblical equality is not hard to find once you take away the veil of patriarchy and search for it.

I bumped into an old friend of mine recently, a veteran pastor and church leader who I know to be a kind-hearted man. Last time I spoke with him he indicated he had become willing to investigate the claims of biblical equality for women. "So did you ever resolve that for yourself?" I asked him as we caught up with each other.

"I'm still mushy on it," he confessed as he waved his hand in an up-down gesture.

"Still in Mushville?" I asked, trying to downplay my incredulity that he was still on the fence after all these years.

"Yes, still in Mushville."

This disappointed me, yet I have faith that he will exit Mushville when he decides to review the overwhelming evidence that the Bible affirms women in all areas of leadership and spiritual authority.

I also have faith that this generation which is like no other, will dismantle the polite oppression of women in the church faster than ever before with the plethora of digital and internet communication. Biblical scholarship can be accessed and transmitted with the mere touch of a button. Those who give themselves over to a spirit of inquiry will find more than enough persuasive information that women are free to teach, preach, lead and partner with men in every sphere. I like to hope that there is a tide of change coming.

I like this tweet I saw posted on Twitter, "When the tidal wave of change comes grab a surfboard."[52] I hope the church will ride this wave as far as it can into a new era of widespread collaboration between women and men of faith in all areas of church, home and society.

PART TWO

RESISTANCE

It's when people leave their place in the social hierarchy that the trouble starts. It's when they start getting uppity and rebellious that they invoke the wrath of the complacent and of the powerful.[53]

Carol Tavris, Social Psychologist

Chapter Six: The Bible Tells Me So {Part Two}

Resisting the male-only voice and image of God

> God created man in His own image, in the image of God He created him; male and female He created them.
>
> Genesis 1:27

> If God is male, than male is God.[54]
>
> Mary Daly, Feminist Philosopher

From the time I was a little girl, God has been uniquely and unequivocally male. I have prayed for decades to God my Father in heaven; images of male heroes and God as a Warrior King dominate nearly all the Bible stories that I've learned and studied over the past thirty years. It has not been lost on me that when Jesus, *the Son* of God, gathered twelve friends to be his inner circle, they were all men. Combine this with the fact that the overwhelming majority of Bible teachers I've had during my entire spiritual journey have also been men.

Even the Christian spirituality books I like to read are mostly authored by men. I once counted the book titles in a catalog from a large mainstream publisher to see how many of their current books had been authored by women. Out of more than 300 titles, a mere fourteen had been written by a woman and even then, two of those had been coauthored with a man.

Modern Christianity, at first glance, is a spiritual path to a male God who gives privilege to the gender blessed with male chromosomes.

This is not a tirade against men. I love men. I was fathered by a man, I married a man and I'm raising a future man. Some of my favorite people are men. I have no squabble with the other sex, but the reality is that the faith of my fathers is just that: a faith of fathers.

A friend of mine who was raised Baptist, but later left the denomination in favor of paganism, said to me that when he took a long, hard look at the faith of his youth, one of the disconcerting questions that emerged for him was this: "Where's the mom?"

Sue Monk Kidd writes about her awakening of the male imagery that saturated her childhood Christian upbringing:

> As the service began, I became acutely aware that every hymn and biblical passage used only masculine pronouns, as if that was all there was. Until then I had accepted that when it said men and brotherhood that somehow meant me, too. But now, in a place much deeper than my head, I didn't feel included at all. I realized that lacking the feminine, the language had communicated to me in subtle ways that women were nonentities; that women counted mostly as they related to men. Until that moment, I'd had no idea just how important language is in forming our lives. What happens to a female when all her life she hears sacred language indirectly, filtered through male terms?[55]

She raises an important question: What does happen to a woman when the spiritual imagery of her life is dominated by male vocabulary?

She might get some fury like my friend Michelle did who said that as a child she became angry at God. "I was pissed that God was a man, that Jesus was a man, I hated that I wasn't a man. I hated my gender."

Hated my gender. That's the thing of it. If women of faith are consistently given a male-only image of God by male-dominated voices, it is going to take a toll on a woman's identity. If this isn't enough, there's also the marginalization that women experience within their faith tribes like exclusion from positions of leadership because of femaleness, being relegated to roles of subservience because of femaleness, and an absence of inclusion in the sacred language of sermons, prayers and songs God because of femaleness.

What do these omissions tell women and men?

One of my friends said at one of my listening parties, "Women are defective. I am defective."

"It's like the God of the Bible doesn't like or support women," said another.

In an online video interview, novelist Anne Rice said of women in the church, "You'd get the impression that Jesus died a little more for men."[56]

Women's self-esteem takes a battering from culture with the saturation of sexual images, but instead of finding refuge in the church, women find confirmation that men do indeed rule the world, as well as the church.

When God's voice and image are repeatedly expressed in male metaphors and terms—Father, Son, He, Him, King, Lord, Prince—how can women not be affected in how they view the Creator and also themselves?

Theologian Elizabeth A. Johnson, author of *She Who Is*, writes:

> ... women internalize the images and notions declared about them by the ruling group and come to believe it of themselves. Being inculturated in a thousand subtle ways through the idea that women are not as capable as men, nor are they expected to be, leads to an internalized sense of powerlessness. The internalization of secondary status then functions like a self-fulfilling prophecy, inculcating low self-esteem, passivity, and an assessment of oneself as inadequate even where that is patently untrue.
>
> This process is strongly aided and abetted by male-centered language and symbol systems...women have been robbed of the power of naming, of naming themselves, the world,

and ultimate holy mystery, having instead to receive the names given by those who rule over them.[57]

To internalize ourselves as having secondary status becomes normal (yet oppressive) when the language we possess about God and our faith excludes the image and voice of women. We unwittingly adopt a concept of God that lacks female characteristics. But to communicate the Person of God as uniquely male is to deify male. It is like saying that though the Creator breathed life into woman, he did so as an afterthought. Women become viewed like leftover scraps of a grand, cosmic art project of the Creator.

If a woman doesn't resist a male-only image of God, she risks her womanhood becoming swallowed whole by a tsunami wave of patriarchal power. She will look to men to define her identity which is exactly what God predicted in the garden of Eden when the first couple veered into darkness with humankind's first step into self-rule. God said to Eve:

I will greatly multiply your pain in childbirth,

in pain you will bring forth children;

yet your desire will be for your husband, and he will rule

over you. (Genesis 3:16)

From this beginning, women have looked to men to inform our identity and our value.

This is part of the consequence of sin. The relationship between the genders became dysfunctional in the fall of humanity and we see it played out throughout the cultures around the world and through the long corridors of time to our present age.

But there is one culture that is meant to be free of this dysfunction and that is the culture of the kingdom of God which the apostle Paul described as being where "there is neither male nor female, for you are all one in Christ Jesus," (Galatians 3:28). There is no sexism in God's kingdom.

Yet Christianized sexism becomes normalized when God is portrayed exclusively in male imagery and voice. It perpetuates the polite oppression of women and inequality when there is a steady stream of male-only images. Gender justice matters very much in how we communicate the Creator to one another.

Our view of God is crucial to how we view ourselves, which is why I am convinced that Christ followers must renew our understanding of God as being more than shrouded in masculine mystery. There is feminine language to claim when we speak of God.

In the contemporary church, feminine images of God have been starved out. I think we are long overdue to revive them for the sake of deepening our understanding of the Creator, but also for affirming the *imago Dei* that is carried by every woman in her personhood.

~~

A few years ago I was having a spiritual conversation with a woman I know. Every time I referred to God with a masculine pronoun she would correct me and replace the word with a feminine pronoun instead. She refused to acknowledge God as uniquely male while I had trouble referring to God with feminine language. It made for somewhat of an awkward conversation.

"He is more compassionate than we realize," I said trying to convey to her in my Christian witness that God loved her. She didn't miss a beat.

"She, not he," she said smiling.

I smiled back. "Ok, She," I said wanting to be agreeable. It's just a pronoun, I told myself. God, I surmised, cannot be contained by a pronoun any more than a river can be contained in a wine glass. Language fails us. And yet it betrays us and forms us and informs us of how to view ourselves, the world and yes, more importantly, how we see the Almighty. Vivian, a close friend of mine who often begins her prayers addressing God as "Father and Mother" says, "It's been important to me to be aware of the pronouns I use."

Language is always going to be limiting. I wrote about this a long while back with a blog entry titled, *Is God a Boy or a Girl?*

> I love language, but quite honestly, as much as language
> thrills me it also frustrates me. It seems to me that the
> limitations of language are the cause of all kinds of
> misunderstanding of who God is and what He/She is
> like.[58]

Words have power, especially words used to express our attempts to understand God as best as we can. Words help us learn, but they can also get in the way. We spend a lot of time as Christians trying to decipher the words of the Bible. We think carefully of our words when we pray and worship. Words are the vehicles by which we transport ideas and knowledge.

Language is like magic, words spun together into ideas and concepts that inspire and inform us of our reality. Especially words that refer to God.

Johnson addresses the challenges of speaking of God. She writes:

> What is the right way to speak about God? This is a
> question of unsurpassed importance, for speech to and
> about the mystery that surrounds human lives and the
> universe itself is a key activity of a community of faith.
> In that speech the symbol of God functions as the primary
> symbol of the whole religious system, the ultimate point
> of reference for understanding experience, life and the
> world.[59]

Johnson points out the importance of language when speaking of God. If our Christian experience is dominated by masculine words when speaking of God, then we are essentially assigning gender to God.

Gender is not bad. I am not suggesting that to use gendered words to relate to God is misguided. But I do think that in the context of the injustice of inequality towards women, that we do well to step back and examine the dominance of male-only imagery for God. Is it accurate? Is it biblical?

To address this means we need to take a look at metaphors. A metaphor is a figure of speech of comparison between two different things that have something in common. Metaphor comes from a Greek word meaning "to transfer or carry over." Metaphors transport meaning from one word picture to another.

I love metaphors. They bring color to stories and vibrancy to concepts. My early growing up years were spent in the South where metaphors run wild throughout the dialect. "It's slower than the second coming of Jesus," said a grandmotherly Southern woman to me one time when I had asked when the next bus was arriving.

The Bible is brimming with metaphor. Jesus himself used plenty of metaphors in his teachings, those little stories that we call parables. When he spoke about birds of the air eating seed from someone's heart, obviously he was using metaphor to get his point across.

There are many different metaphors in the Old and New Testaments that are used when referencing God. He is like a high tower (Proverbs 18:10), or a rock and a fortress (2 Samuel 22:2). God is described as a warrior (Exodus 15:3) and also a husband (Jeremiah 31:32). The Psalmist used many images when speaking of God such as a shield (Psalm 3:3), a cup (Psalm 16:5), a horn (Psalm 18:2), and of course, a shepherd (Psalm 23:1). These are only a few examples of the use of metaphor when describing God. At best, though, they can only reveal fragments of the Divine Creator. Not whole pieces.

Blogger and author Julie Clawson writes:

> The nature of language is that words are not the thing in itself, but a description or symbol of that thing. Words are finite and limited to our experience. So an infinite God cannot fully be defined by words. But God has been partially revealed in terms that we can understand through our experiences. Metaphors are used – objects, ideas, gender - to describe God. In using the metaphors

we are saying that God is a bit like these things I am able to understand.[60]

But what of gender? Do biblical references of God as father and other masculine titles reveal God as having a masculine nature? Or is gender yet another metaphor in an effort to define this Infinite Being whose existence surpasses our understanding and imagination?

Theologian R.K. McGregor Wright writes that "Gendered imagery for God is metaphorical language,"[61] and that projecting gender onto God is to "turn the divine into human."[62] Wright also points out that pagan deities are gendered, but the God of the Bible is not like an idol.[63] Sexuality is not a defining characteristic of the Creator as it is for gods and goddesses.

The birth of Jesus does not indicate that God is male any more than it indicates that God is Jewish. The incarnation of God in Jesus is the incarnation of God in human form rather than male form.

Aida Besancon Spencer, a New Testament scholar and writer, explains it this way:

> The Bible linguistically and theologically highlights the importance of understanding Jesus first and primarily as human. That he was male is also true, but that fact should never be said to reflect God's sexuality. Jesus' maleness was a limitation imposed on the incarnate God, not a reflection of God's essence.[64]

Women can breathe a sigh of relief that God in revealing himself through Jesus was not emphasizing maleness in his nature. God coming in Person was the point.

Spencer also writes:

> Masculine biblical language for God refers to grammatical, not natural, gender. God is the source of everything, including gender. Therefore, males and females are both needed to reflect God's image. Consequently, God is identified with a variety of characteristics and culturally

gendered roles of both females and males, identifying with both genders.[65]

God's image is revealed through both male and female human beings while he remains God without possessing human sexuality. I appreciate this, and I have become awed by the wonderment that the Creator gives us clues about his nature through human gender.

If God is to be found in male and female imagery and metaphors, and if terms like father, Lord and king are mere symbols to hint at God's essence, then, like my friend asked so many years ago, "Where's the mom?" Where then is the feminine language of God in the Bible and where is it in the church?

The absence of female imagery is an absence of female voice and female power. Women of faith accept this as normal, as if the Deity of our religion is only a Father who favors his sons to lead the way. A woman as subservient is all she knows since she has been marginalized since she was born and born again. This is how women remain oppressed, no matter how kindly that oppression might look.

So ... where is the mom?

Let's go find her.

~~

"You have got to read this book," said my friends Fran and Len handing me a cheesy looking Christian novel.

"I don't usually read novels," I mumbled as they thrust it into my hands anyway.

"Just read it," they insisted.

The book was called *The Shack*, written by Paul Young, a friend of theirs who lives in the Portland area. The story centers on a character named Mack, a man who lives with great sadness after the kidnapping and brutal murder of his young daughter during a family camping trip. Several years later Mack receives a divine invitation to meet up with God at the same shack where his daughter's bloody dress had been found. Mack travels to the shack with understandable trepidation, but when God finally shows up, she appears to Mack as a jovial African-American woman who likes to be called Papa:

> "Mackenzie, I am neither male nor female, even though both genders are derived from my nature. If I choose to appear to you as a man or a woman, it's because I love you. For me to appear to you as a woman and suggest that you call me Papa is simply to mix metaphors, to help you keep from falling so easily back into your religious conditioning."[66]

The Shack went on to sell over 12 million copies and as a result, attracted a large amount of attention and critique. The story resonated deeply with many Christians despite the unconventional portrayal of God the Father as a black woman. But many critics took issue with the book, which wrestles with layers of theological treatises as well as conceptions of what God's nature is like.

One of the most controversial themes of *The Shack* is the portrayal of God in the feminine. One reviewer wrote that *The Shack* promoted goddess worship by using a female character to depict God. To prove his point, he quoted the second of the Ten Commandments, "You shall have no other gods before me," (Exodus 20:3) and accused the author of creating an idolatrous image of God with a female image.

Another reviewer, a theologian at a conservative seminary, wrote that this feminized version of God and the book's soaring popularity with Christians was proof of the infiltration of feminism in the church. One pastor at a large church here in the Pacific Northwest went so far as to tell his congregation to avoid reading the book.

One conservative Christian bookstore owner expressed outrage and even asked me to leave his store when he overheard me tell another customer where the book could be found since he refused to carry it in his shop. Such was the extent of controversy over a novel that had the audacity to portray the Creator as a woman.

I had a chance to interview the author several times. In one particular interview, I angled my focus on the decision Paul made as a storyteller to present God the Father as a black woman named Papa:

> Pam: In your novel, *The Shack*, you choose to use a female character to portray God the Father. How does this artistic choice in character development reveal your perspective on gender and the triune God?
>
> Paul: My journey into the nature of the Trinity actually began by my exploration of the issues of gender. I have spent about 25 years working on questions related to maleness and femaleness and if you spend enough time investigating such questions, you will invariably find yourself focused on the nature of God and on the Trinity. You discover, of course, that God is neither male nor female, but both genders derive their identity from the nature of God. God is Spirit and both genders reflect the image of God. So the use of imagery, male or female, is always going to be inadequate.
>
> However, Scripture abounds with both male and female imagery for God, bridges to help us understand God's magnificent character and nature. In part I wanted to defy some of the existing paradigms regarding gender.[67]

The firestorm over Paul's choice to use a female character to portray God more than reveals how obscured our vision of God has become. The church has not only forgotten the mother heart of God but is apparently also offended by it!

The Shack was not being unbiblical in using a feminine metaphor for God. The Bible itself actually has many. We don't have to look very far to find feminine references to the Creator.

In Genesis 1:2 we read, "The earth was formless and void, and darkness was over the surface of the deep, and the Spirit of God was moving over the surface of the waters." This is a beautiful, poetic description of the birth of creation.

What is interesting to note is that the Hebrew word for "moving" is *ruach,* a word that has feminine gender. All Hebrew nouns have either a masculine or feminine gender though it does not mean the word refers to male or female.[68] *Ruach* is a feminine word which of itself does not mean a whole lot, but this same word is also used in Deuteronomy 32:11:

> Like an eagle that stirs up its nest, that hovers over its
> young, he spread his wings and caught them, he carried
> them on his pinions.

This metaphor of God is clearly maternal, and what is worth paying attention to is how the word *ruach* is being used: first, in the birth of creation and then again in reference to describing God with feminine imagery. What is the language trying to tell us about God?

In Exodus 34 we have the story of God revealing and speaking of himself to Moses from Mount Sinai. As God passes by Moses he declares of himself, "The Lord, the Lord God, compassionate and gracious, slow to anger and abounding in lovingkindness and truth." The word compassion in Hebrew (*rahamim*) has as its root, *rehem*, the word for womb.[69] Again, feminine imagery is woven into the language to help explain what God is like.

She Who Is references feminist biblical scholar and theologian, Phyllis Trible, in explaining the significance of these feminine root Hebrew words:

> ... the word for woman's womb and the word for
> compassion are cognates, both further related to the verb
> to show mercy and the adjective merciful.
> In its singular form the noun *rehem* means "womb" or
> "uterus." In the plural, *rahamim*, this concrete meaning
> spans to the abstraction of compassion, mercy and
> love...70

This makes for a powerful, feminine metaphor. Here we have God saying of himself that he is compassionate, a term whose taproot is womb, an intimate and feminine image for the God of the universe to apply to himself.

What does this reveal about the God of the Bible? I am inspired when I think of how male and female are made in his image, and though God does not possess gender as human beings do, the Creator communicates the beauty and mystery of what he is like through both male and female characteristics.

It is astounding to me that I have lived for many years in all kinds of church circles and yet have been deprived of hearing sermons or teachings or worship songs and prayers that use female language to honor God. Yet God himself used feminine language to describe himself.

These cited examples I've provided are obviously just an introduction of how feminine imagery is found on the underside of the tapestry of the Bible. "The Mom" is found throughout the Scriptures, hidden in the roots of biblical words, and obscured by the dominance of male language and symbols.

Johnson writes:

> Language about God in female images not only challenges the literal mindedness that has clung to male images in inherited God-talk; it not only questions their dominance in discourse about holy mystery. But insofar as "the symbol gives rise to thought," such speech calls into question prevailing structures of patriarchy…[71]

Patriarchal language cloaks the maternal heart of God. We need to remove the filter of God-as-a-male-god for our vision of God to expand.

There are many examples of God being described with feminine metaphors throughout the Bible. Here are a few:

Deuteronomy 32:11 Like a mother eagle

Deuteronomy 32:18 Like one who gives birth

Psalm 22:9 Like a midwife

Isaiah 42:14 Like a woman in labor

Isaiah 49:15 Like a nursing mother

Isaiah 66:13 Like a comforting mother

Hosea 13:8 Like a mother bear

Matthew 23:37 Like a mother hen

The "Mom" is not so hard to find. She is to be found in the sacred Scriptures, and she is also to be found in the prayers and utterances among believers from the past.

Many saints throughout history have referred to God as both Mother and Father. One early church father is recorded as praying, "Thou art my Father, thou art my Mother, thou my Brother, thou art Friend ... "[72] Clement of Alexandria referred to God in the masculine and the feminine writing, "In his ineffable essence he is father; in his compassion to us he became mother."[73] Julian of Norwich wrote, "As truly as God is our Father, so is truly God our Mother."[74]

They were not praying to two gods, as if the Creator is a male deity as well as female deity. As was noted earlier, the pagan gods were male or female and were sexually active in the myths and lore of their followers. But the God of the Hebrews and of the Christians is One God, revealed in humankind through the two genders of male and female, yet as One Divine Being.

We must remember that God is neither male nor female. Scripture is clear on this point. In John 4:24 Jesus said, "God is spirit." Human metaphors about the Divine are only that- metaphors. Shadowy comparisons to help us wrap our finite minds around the existence of this Infinite Being. It is only one mystery of many in our pursuit of knowing who God is and what he is like.

But the great truth here is that God did, after all, create male and female, and with equal power and voice. The first man was never given authority over the first woman as if he bore a greater degree of the image of God. For when God created Adam, Eve was already there, lurking beneath in Adam's flesh and bones. She waited to be birthed from him, to be called out of hiding by the Creator. Adam was one man, yet he carried the image of woman within like buried treasure.

When God called her out from beneath Adam's side, it was to bring Adam a companion like himself. Eve was never designated as the lesser sex nor the helper gender in the sense of being assigned a divine role of servitude to men. That idea comes from patriarchal thinking.

When Eve made her entrance into the world, Genesis 2 tells us that Adam looked upon her and uttered the first recorded human sentence, which is found in verse 23:

This is now bone of my bones, and flesh of my flesh; she
shall be called woman, because she was taken out of man.

Scholars say that Adam uses the Hebrew *ish* for man and *isha* for woman, a play on words, as the first man viewed the first woman and understood she was the same as he, but distinct.[75] Different in appearance, yet the same in design. She was the *isha* to his *ish*, the female version of the single humanity made after the image of God. Not as an afterthought. Womankind, from the beginning, has been esteemed by the Creator with as much love and regard as man.

But throughout my many years as a Christ follower, there has been an overwhelming absence of storytelling and preaching of woman in the image of God and God in the image of woman. We do not acknowledge the mother heart of God because we do not even know that She is there. Or if allow ourselves to wonder about feminine language for God and motherly imagery, we concern ourselves that we might be headed into a heretical wilderness.

Sue Monk Kidd writes that there is a "real and undeniable connection between the repression of feminine in our deity and the repression of women ... The fear of and resistance to feminine images goes deep."[76] We need to ignore these fears and be willing to trek into the wild to rediscover the motherly presence of God.

Once as a new Christian I prayed to God as mother out loud at a home Bible study. The small group I huddled with in prayer was mixed with men and women. As I uttered the words, "Dear Mother in heaven," one of the men snorted, a kind of half chuckle, half grunt with absurdity melting off his lips. It was like getting burned with candle wax. It startled me. I opened my eyes, raising them to see the man staring at me with a flame of challenge in his glare. I felt a rise of shame inside of me. Did I err in addressing the Creator as Mother? Had I done something wrong?

I cannot even recall why it is that I felt inspired to pray to God as Mother in the first place, but in the moment it seemed right. It seemed natural. But I had crossed some kind of line into unfamiliar territory.

What my young, newly converted heart had unknowingly stumbled upon, was the ancient burial ground of God as woman. She'd been buried long ago, and in Her place reigned Male Supreme. By resurrecting her in prayer as Mother, I had provoked the patriarchal spirit which immediately sought to silence me through my praying brother's disapproval. And it worked. I ran away, or rather, the feminine spirit inside of me ran away from God as mother.

It would be another two decades before I could address my Creator as Mother again. But there She was, waiting for me alongside my Father. All along, God my Mother had watched over me until I found my way back home.

Chapter Seven: Half the Justice

Halfway to equality gets us nowhere

Half measures availed us nothing. We stood at the turning point.[77]

Alcoholics Anonymous

When it comes to the cause of justice, I take no prisoners and I don't believe in compromise.

Mary Frances Berry

When Jerry and I married in Hong Kong, we went to an island off the southern coast of Thailand for our honeymoon. One day we joined an excursion that explored smaller, remote islands in the area. At one stop, we were directed to hike a path to the highest point of the island. The tour guides said that we would be rewarded with a gorgeous view of the Gulf of Thailand.

Jerry and I trudged up the hill with about three dozen other tourists. It was very hot, the tropical air thick and humid. Sweat oozed down my face stinging my eyes. The path cut through a jungle of thick, green foliage. It was like walking through a canyon of impenetrable green walls. I began to tire. My legs were getting heavier with each step forward. "I can't do it," I said to Jerry. "Let's turn back."

We were the first ones to return to the waiting boat. Less than an hour later, the others arrived back, chattering with excitement about the incredible view from the top of the island. To this day Jerry and I do not know what we missed since we only made it halfway.

Halfway got us nowhere.

It is like that for many women in many churches - half measures of justice that women accept in the face of inequality in church. Instead of pressing on to the pinnacle of mutuality between the sexes, women opt to settle for what they've got, a compromise of go along to get along.

There's a popular church that has a well-developed social justice ministry. They are an active force of good in their community. Their fellowship includes esteemed men and women who are highly accomplished such as theologians, business people, writers and artists. It is a beautiful, compelling spiritual community. There's just one little detail that I find disconcerting: the way they treat their women.

Women are not allowed within this church to possess their full personhood. Women serve in so many ways except in the upper chambers of church leadership. Those offices are for men only. Women may exercise their gifting and voice up to a point, such as leading other women and children, but men alone are cast in the starring roles with women predictably cast in supporting roles. It is an old, tired storyline.

And yet this church does so much good, especially in the cause of social justice. They have people involved in combating sex trafficking and teams helping with missions overseas to help those who suffer under unjust economic systems. Yet in their own faith community the injustice of inequality towards women continues to go unchecked. It is a paradox when such churches and denominations engage in social justice ministry, yet commit injustice by discriminating women.

Many churches justify their discriminatory treatment towards women with Scripture as well as a dismissive shrug. Women are taught to remain content in subservient roles and to let go of selfish ambitions for greater leadership.

Some faith tribes signal their women that to desire greater influence is to desire something dysfunctional. Women are told to be grateful for what they have and to focus on what they can do rather than what they can't. But this is unjust and it is also demeaning to half the church's population. When a woman does awaken to swirl of inequity, she may feel self-seeking for questioning the status quo, as if her desire for equality is an exercise of misplaced ambition. It is further confusing if a woman's faith community serves others well, especially in social justice ministries. How can a woman indulge feelings of being slighted and marginalized if her church is otherwise stellar in ministry and mission? She talks herself into letting it go, ignore the injustice of inequality, for to make a fuss over it risks sounding self-absorbed and self-seeking.

A friend of mine brought this up when we were talking about women and equality in the church. "What about Jesus' call to lay down our rights?" she asked. "Didn't Paul say that Jesus himself did not consider equality a thing to be grasped?"

"Equality with God," I corrected her. "And no, we cannot justify injustice by telling those who are oppressed to just accept it in a spirit of sacrifice. Would we tell that to slaves? Would we tell them to forget about their rights?"

"No," she conceded, "I get your point."

Psychologist Polly Young-Eisendrath addresses this question about women and self-preservation:

> Women agonize over a single question—Am I too selfish?—struggling with the belief that focusing on ourselves is selfish when it comes to spiritual or religious issues. We've been taught that we're inferior to men in our ability to be pure-hearted and wise. [78]

This is one reason of many why women make do with what we have, with the half measures of equality. We wonder if our discontentment and perception of discrimination is simply our own issue. Are we being selfish? Ungrateful? Divisive?

Our person and character comes under scrutiny rather than focusing on the injustice of inequality in the church. Instead of confronting the wrongness of Christian sexism, women are confronted for being dissatisfied and unhappy. There is even at times a pointing of the finger that women who strive for equality are just power hungry.

One church brought to my attention has communicated to its congregation that the struggle for equality is a struggle for control. They're right, but instead of acknowledging the dehumananizing affect of relegating women to subservience, they blame women for seeking mutuality with their men.

Like the commenter who left this remark at my blog:

> There are thousands of ministry opportunities and the one
> that women are not permitted to pursue, they want! Why
> is that? [79]

The commenter betrays his or her view of women in that women are expected to be content with what they already have. Be content with this measure of equality, which I define as being a half measure of justice. And like my abandoned hike to the top of the island, half measures of justice don't get women to the destination of equality with their brothers in Christ.

It was this kind of rhetoric that kept the Jim Crow laws of the South empowered for years. Law abiding citizens, including Christians, were able in good conscience to live in communities that had signs posted like *Whites Only*, or *No Colored People* at movie theaters and restaurants. There was also the infamous bus law that required black passengers to give up their seat to a white passenger if all seats were taken.

How effectual would it have been if during the Civil Rights movement when these laws were challenged activists conceded in compromise? Which right would be compromised? Which right would be laid down by blacks in an effort to preserve the peace?

It is ludicrous to put the responsibility of making nice with oppressive conditions on the oppressed themselves. It would have been a half measure that would have availed nothing had Civil Rights activists negotiated which Jim Crow laws to maintain in order to enjoy the liberty of others.

Churches that "allow women" to lead in certain pastoral roles, but ban them from others due to gender are acting in the spirit of Jim Crow, not the Spirit of Jesus. I believe churches that keep women caged with stained glass barriers are not fulfilling the scriptural mandate of justice nor biblical equality. It is a half measure when half the church is allowed to be heard to some degree, but relegated to the back pews in others because they don't have the correct chromosomes.

Bishop Desmond Tutu once said, "I am not interested in picking up crumbs of compassion thrown from the table of someone who considers himself my master. I want the full menu of rights."[80] I like that, and I hope that a tide of resistance among women and men will gain momentum in refusing half measures of equality.

Jesus said, "You will know the truth and the truth will set you free," (John 8:32). Not half truths. The whole truth, and nothing but the truth, which is this: Women are to be afforded full personhood in all corners and roles of the spiritual community known as church. Anything less, like meeting halfway, is just that, a half measure that avails a woman partial liberty, which is not true liberty. It's an illusion of compromise and diplomacy.

The injustice of inequality takes its toll on women, like my friend Mimi whom I'll introduce you to. She tried to work it out her whole life, but in the end, a half measure of justice felt like no measure at all.

~~

I met my friend Mimi at The Bridge, a non-denominational church in Portland famous for its raucous worship music and young, indy crowd. Mimi and I were among a handful who are over the age of forty. Before coming to The Bridge, Mimi had been on staff at a megachurch for seventeen years. I eventually learned Mimi's whole story of why she walked away from her church and her salaried church position. It is a textbook case of Christianized sexism veiled in ambiguity and half measures of equality.

Mimi, who grew up in a conservative denomination, remembers that as a little girl she knew that if she had been born a boy she would grow up to be a preacher. But since God saw fit to give her girl parts, she did not think this was an option for her future. Even though she lacked the correct plumbing, her bent for leadership ebbed its presence through the crevices and cracks of her life.

"I was always enthralled with the church," she told me, her Tennessee southern drawl rolling the words out of her mouth. She left Tennessee many years ago for the Pacific Northwest, and though you can take the woman out of the South you can't take the South out of the woman, which is why I tend to get my drawl on when I am around Mimi. I spent my early years growing up in the magnolia groves of central Louisiana.

Mimi and I always enjoy reliving our common southern heritage of sweet tea and buttermilk fried chicken. "Weren't you told not to act ugly?" I asked as we compared our upbringing. Acting ugly is a southern mother's way of telling her children to not misbehave. Sometimes when I personify the inequality of women in the church, she comes at me like a ghost of a southern woman in a bonnet (go figure) holding a Big Bible under her arm, whilst she wags her finger and scolds me, "Stop acting ugly, Pam, and obey the Word." Shame in a bonnet. I guess she shows up in all kinds of guises with all sorts of dialects and accents.

With all that leadership and pastoral gifting in her bones aching for relief, Mimi began a Bible study that met on Saturday mornings. She was in junior high school. "I knew I wouldn't get the ok as a girl to run something like this so I talked the preacher's son into leading it with me so we'd get a yes. But I was the one who was really leading it."

Her parents had no issue with their daughter teaching a Bible study, but one of the leaders of the church approached her father and chided him, "You're letting her rule the roost."

Thus, the ghost of shame shifted through the churchman who challenged her father's honor for allowing Mimi to exercise public leadership. Such tensions are not uncommon at all for female Christ followers and their families.

This incident and others like it served to download a childhood of messaging to Mimi that girls need to remain submissive and that public service and preaching were better left to men. Shame and confusion swirled around her developing identity as she sorted out what desires she was allowed to have. "Admitting to myself and especially out loud to others that I wanted to lead and teach was like saying I wanted to be a prostitute," jokes Mimi with her signature dry sense of humor.

Mimi grew into womanhood and then married and moved away from the denomination of her youth. She discovered a new faith community that seemed to esteem women in ministry. It was a much freer atmosphere than the church of her childhood. Mimi's gifting was quickly recognized and soon, she was on the staff payroll of her new church.

The staff grew, the responsibilities grew, but unfortunately, the opportunities did not. Mimi began to fill stifled again, but in a different kind of way than the rigid traditionalistic religion of her youth.

Mimi led in various ways—always among children and youth—and though she adored serving the kids in her church, she often felt the tension of an invisible boundary line that she was not allowed to cross. No one told her she couldn't do certain things because of being a woman, but she felt it, an indefinable unease that over time came into focus. She determined to make the best of her staff position.

She became an outstanding children's pastor, but secretly she longed to lead in a more public and broader way. Her roles of leadership in the church were always behind the scenes. She watched male fellow staff members given opportunities to serve the church at large, yet she remained in the background. It was beginning to seem like discrimination.

Mimi felt hesitant on calling out these issues of inequality. It was risky. "It's like trying to take your clothes off if you say what you really think," she says.

Many of the men on church staff regularly rotated on the preaching schedule, but not Mimi. Her ideas, though, when voiced at staff meetings, sometimes showed up packaged and preached on a Sunday morning. Ironically, she could spark others to teach, though she herself was disallowed from the pulpit.

What if she was a man, she'd wonder, would she have more influence and leadership? Or was it just her? Was it a lack of gifting ... or was it inequality? In her heart she knew the ugly truth and the knowing of it made her feel devalued and to some extent, insignificant. "It felt like I couldn't be the one I was made to be," says Mimi.

There were other women who came and went on staff, though never as senior leadership. "As long as you served kids you were fine," reports Mimi.

She knew she was good at leading the kids, but she also knew that she would thrive in other areas of ministry in the church. The problem was the same old story she had known from her girlhood: women keep secondary roles while men hold primary roles.

There have been so many women I know like Mimi who are left to second-guess their abilities because of their church's patriarchal structure and the half measures of equality offered women.

The insistence to relegate church roles based on gender, rather than gifting has meant the minimizing of untold numbers of women solely because of their femininity. It has blurred the vision of many others who silently endure inequality and injustice because they are unconvinced that they are truly oppressed by the great web of patriarchal lies.

The lack of conviction for equality for women is further deepened by the illusion that equality already exists. Half measures of justice are mistaken for full measures. Feminist and activist Gloria Steinem famously said, "The first resistance to social change is to say it's not necessary." The church is divided about women's equality because many don't think it is necessary.

The teaching gift inside of Mimi remained hidden, waiting for opportunity to speak and preach to the congregation even though it was understood women just did not preach in this church. She would scold herself, "Just let it go."

The unrelenting corrosion of Christianized sexism pushed Mimi past her breaking point, and she at long last gave her church her two weeks' notice. There was no final straw moment. Just a quiet revolution that had been raging inside of her for years that she could no longer ignore. She could not in good conscience continue to serve a system that kept women in subservient roles. But even as she departed, she wondered if her perception was accurate. Perhaps all the years of being passed over had nothing to do with gender.

Mimi determined to stay in fellowship with her church after she resigned from her position, despite the ambiguity she had endured for nearly two decades. "It was like being in a relationship with a passive-aggressive man," says Mimi. She committed to remaining nice and ladylike in order to preserve unity. "I was terrified of causing an upset. But the next Sunday my replacement was on the platform, this inexperienced young man they had hired to replace me, and he was serving communion ... and doing it poorly," she says with a wry chuckle. "So I quit going to church after that. I couldn't keep going and making nice and pretending that I was alright with this system of mistreating women."

And just like that, after nearly twenty years of doing life with a community church filled with good people she cared for, Mimi walked away. It wasn't easy, and it wasn't glorious, but it was freeing. "I just couldn't keep pretending anymore," she recounts. "It felt good to stop trying to make it work."

There are many reasons why Mimi endured the injustice of inequality in her church for as long as she did. The people were nice. They were her friends. Her family was deeply rooted in the fabric of the church. It was her paid position. And there were, after all, opportunities for women to serve and lead to a certain point, though not to the degree as men, but opportunities did exist.

This is how half measures of justice paralyze women into enduring circumstances of sexism. A woman of faith has to deal with the internal battle of her own perceptions and convictions. Is she experiencing inequality? And if so, what of it? This is where the heart of the struggle lies for a woman. She has to discover for herself what she believes and whether or not she will resist the unjust practice of inequality in church. Doing so is not easy. There is always the temptation to trivialize discrimination as a harmless, archaic church tradition. But it's not. Just ask Mimi.

~~

Women the world over are experts at trivializing the inequity that pushes us back. We do this because we are conditioned to do so. We are brought up within and apart from the church to be accommodating, to give preference to others at the expense of our own thoughts and desires. It is a complicated mess of concepts that any woman awakening to her feminine power must contend with.

The struggle for equity for women is an internal struggle. It is a tug of war not with men, nor with patriarchal systems, but with ourselves. We remain marginalized for we are fairly convinced that this is where we are meant to be. Or worse, that the equality we long for is not really that important, that it's a distraction to the mission of the church. We make light of inequality out of a misguided sense of duty.

Sue Monk Kidd writes:

> Trivializing our experiences is a very old and shrewd way of controlling ourselves. We do it by censoring our expressions of truth or viewing them as inconsequential. We learned the technique from a culture that has practiced it like an art form.[81]

When Christian women trivialize our experiences of inequality, we often do it with the idea that we are being selfless and Christlike. Aren't we supposed to lay down our rights? Aren't we supposed to have servant hearts and not be ambitious? That's why I shriveled up inside those years ago when my friend disapproved of my feminism with her story of the missionary who laid down her rights so a man could lead instead. I felt trivialized, as if the very desire for justice and equity between men and women was wrong.

I minimized my desire for women to be recognized as equal when I felt shamed by my friend. But in trivializing the issue of equality, I inadvertently minimized myself.

I think Mimi did the same thing by arguing herself out of the building without a word. There is a Chinese proverb that says, "Women hold up half the sky." What a picture of collaboration for women and men to hold up the sky together. Yet in many churches today women are conditioned that we are not meant to hold up the sky. We are meant to serve those who do.

Women minimize inequality as we compromise our personhood to keep the peace. What we're really saying is, "I am petty and unimportant. I'm trivial and inconsequential." This is the fall-out of accepting half measures of justice. It is not a road that will lead to full equality for women in the church.

I asked a woman I know about women and equality at her church. She said, "I have always been free to lead and minister in whatever God calls me to. Whenever I ask the pastor about doing something he always says yes."

"Are women co-leading the church as pastors or elders?" I asked.

"No, men are the elders and pastors, but women, even though they don't hold these positions have a lot of influence and leadership. It's just behind the scenes. The elder's wives give their husbands a lot of perspective and insight. Women do lead the church and do have a voice. It's just not as obvious."

As I pressed the conversation, it became apparent that she was content with the way things were. I, on the other hand, began to feel like a whiny ungrateful woman who was likely operating in a wounded spirit. It adds to the confusion when other women seem fine with the very thing that flares indignation within me. It also flares up my insecurities as well as my pride.

The human need for belonging and approval is powerful. Dissent threatens acceptance. This is another factor weaved into the tapestry of a woman's complicit role in accepting half measures of justice. She doesn't want to cause an upset, as Mimi put it, for it casts an ominous shadow over the security of having a place to belong.

~~

The oppression of women in the church, past and present, has been apparent in untold numbers across the ages. For the better part of Christianity, women have been assigned roles as lesser than and for much of history women have possessed a gentle acquiescence to being marginalized. Silent consent is much easier than making a fuss. Such silence and acceptance to the way things are gives the impression that all is well. Women show up to church each week and maintain their volunteer obligations in serving and a vast array of other commitments they've taken on to help their church community thrive. Women are the unsung heroes on Sunday morning, the workforce of keeping the church flowing and humming week after week.

In many faith communities, there are no conversations about the inequality of women. We lack an awareness of the oppression of patriarchal culture upon a woman's identity and life, or worse, a tacit agreement to keep the status quo and not engage in critical thought or language. So many good Christian women have been domesticated by being told countless times in a myriad of ways that a submissive woman is a godly woman, that a quiet, well-behaved female is pleasing to God. Many churched women won't challenge the male-dominated system they find themselves in for this would smack of divisiveness.

Then there are other women who find themselves deep in critical thought over the mess of relationships and inequity between the genders in the kingdom of Jesus. They have experienced an awakening of some kind, as I did, when my friend Tracey in Hong Kong led me to the wide, open meadow of women being equally capable and called. This was a significant shift in my story. The misogynistic threads began to loosen and unravel. This process took more than a decade for me to completely awaken to the rampant inequality that runs throughout the church. The fog of vagueness made it hard to distinguish.

In one of the first churches I participated in as a young adult, women seemed to be in collaboration with men. A man would give the sermon, while a woman was likely playing the piano at the same service. Men led Bible studies and missions trips, but women were right there, leading in supportive roles, but leading just the same. I never at that time would have characterized the churches I worshipped in as places of inequality. But then again, it was never blatant.

I have several friends who are members of denominations that ordain women. "But where are the women?" they ask when they survey the churchscape in search of evidence of equality.

There are many churches and denominations that sound like they are equal opportunity faith communities, but in practice they are not. "If you can't be kind, at least be vague," says journalist Judith Manners. This could be the slogan for many churches who do not permit women to fully engage in their gifting. Vagueness keeps women guessing as to what's really going on. Vague understanding of policy and practice keeps those without power, powerless; vague understanding keeps those in power, empowered. A vague feeling or understanding of the injustice of inequality keeps patriarchy empowered.

Like one church we participated in for a few years. The senior pastor insisted that women were free to be and do whatever God's call on their lives was, yet there was not a single woman among the elders or on staff as a teaching pastor. Women, though, did possess key positions as women's ministry leaders and Sunday school teachers. Much of the volunteer work force was comprised of women. It gave an allure of mutuality between men and women and to a certain degree this was true. But there was an unclear boundary.

Vagueness keeps the powerless, powerless. It's what kept Mimi in her church for so many years. There was not clear communication that she could not attain greater influence or higher positions of church leadership due to her female rank. It was inferred; she felt it inferred and saw it surface from time to time in crystal clear clarity. But there was no straight talk about women and position. Just a thick stained glass ceiling that glowed with possibility.

Ambiguity becomes the murky curtain by which true equality is trapped behind. Shadowy understanding about what our faith communities believe and esteem about women—and what we believe about ourselves— keeps women guessing. Worse, it produces indifference. Women remain unconcerned. Indifference settles in with paralyzing power.

Writer Joan Vinge says: "Indifference is the strongest force in the universe. It makes everything it touches meaningless. Love and hate don't stand a chance against it."

Vague understanding breeds indifference. If women and men better understood the insidious nature of inequality, surely there would be a greater outcry of injustice.

Imagine our daughters attending schools taught entirely by men. Imagine our daughters being told from kindergarten through their senior year in high school that men have been ordained by society to lead them intellectually and vocationally. Imagine our daughters believing it, for this is what they have been taught to believe about society.

I think we would be protesting in the streets and pulling our daughters out of those schools, yet this is the same culture we inhabit at church. It's unthinkable to imagine being indifferent and immobilized by such a grave injustice to our daughters. And yet this is what happens to many women in Christendom. We are indifferent to our own oppression and thus, we remain domesticated, docile and so very ladylike with our quiet and submissive spirit that we're told is pleasing to God.

A friend of mine says she's waiting for the day someone sues the church for the way women are discriminated against. I hope that won't happen and yet is that what it's going to take? No matter how hard the journey is, I hope women of faith will keep trudging up the trail towards the destination of equality and not settle for halfway. Halfway gets us nowhere.

Chapter Eight: Breaking Through the Stained Glass Ceiling of Silence

Resisting inequality from the inside out

> I have never been able to find out precisely what feminism is. I only know that people call me a feminist when I express sentiments that differentiate me from a doormat or a prostitute.[82]

Rebecca West, British Writer and Journalist

The stained glass ceiling. It's a clever twist on the metaphor in reference to the glass ceiling women encounter in the workforce. Women of faith encounter stained glass versions that are fortified with Scriptural mandates and patriarchal thinking.

Like a woman I met years ago who felt called to be a pastor when she was in middle school. She mentioned it to her mother who told her, "No, you can't be a pastor since you're a girl. Only men are called to lead in the church." That budding adolescent hit her stained glass ceiling early and hard. It would take years before she was able to crash through and follow the call of God on her life.

There are many concrete examples like this of women being thwarted from ministry and church positions simply because of their gender. I've told some of them, and I know I've only barely scratched the surface. The injustice of inequality towards women in the church has many untold tales.

But another aspect of the stained glass ceiling syndrome is the affect it has on women who aren't pastors or ministry leaders. Women like me. For us, it is an inner stained glass ceiling we must contend with. Not an outer one. The obstacles we face in realizing the women God made us to be are internalized. Beliefs like submission and female subservience, male rule and headship, these beliefs become glued together in a thick mosaic that becomes our lens to view the world. More importantly, it becomes the lens by which we view ourselves as well as one another.

A few years ago I was sitting in a conservative church in Portland. The leaders were all male and the women were just fine with that. For a time I attended a women's Bible study led by one of the pastor's wives. She decided to facilitate on the topic of women. "What does the Bible say about women?" she asked.

We had homework every week. Our facilitator, who possessed a very strong teaching gift and who was married to one of our pastors, prepared lessons for us and handouts of questions as well as assigned reading each week. She did a great job with structuring the study. Her assignments were on topics like submission, spiritual authority, and a woman's role in the home and in the church.

My stomach swirled with tightness each week from the anxiety of this women's group. I privately held the viewpoint that women were free to do anything. I knew I was in the minority. I knew that my perspective would be met with resistance and that I'd be expected to defend it "with Scripture." The tension for me was that I liked these women. I wanted their approval, I wanted to belong and be validated as a woman of God in search of truth and justice.

Dr Brene Brown says that shame is the fear of disconnection, the fear of being "perceived as flawed and unworthy of acceptance or belonging."[83] Attending a Bible study that perpetuated the belief that women must submit to men's authority by virtue of God's word, stirred up deep feelings within me to be authentic yet also to be accepted among the sisterhood. I was nervous that if I was honest about what I really believed about women, that I would be deemed as less than a biblical Christian.

I respected this group of women, including the leader who had a strong personality that emanated a challenging, "Don't Mess with the Bible or Else" kind of aura. She commanded the room when she spoke and many of the women felt intimidated to disagree with her. I admired her spunk. She had passion and conviction and was determined to help influence other women to honor their biblically mandated womanly roles and honor men to do the same. The group's approval and acceptance was important to me. But so was being honest to what my own convictions were.

Each week I diligently studied, pulling out my books about women and leadership, pouring over commentaries and looking up verses and passages. I knew I was going upstream from just about every other woman at that study. I wouldn't shy back, I determined, but I also knew I had to "go in low," with humility and deference for her leadership of the study. I would not debate, I vowed. More than anything else, I did not want to operate in a spirit of divisiveness. In the world of Pentecostals, women who are bitchy or divisive (or strong-minded and independent) are labeled "Jezebel," an Old Testament reference to a queen who had it out with Hebrew prophets. I did not want to be a Jezebel.

I kept that standard the entire time. I often spoke up, but only when called on. I did not interrupt other women even when they said things that were difficult for me to hear. Like one woman who was concerned that America's moral crisis is partly because women are taking leadership away from men. "We wouldn't have all these issues like divorce and society's values nose diving if women and men stayed in the roles that God gave them. Women trying to lead over men confuses our children," said the woman. Many in the study group nodded in assent with her, while I sat there, tension churning in my belly as I witnessed women I respect give agreement that women need to stay out of leadership.

I spoke up sometimes, ever so diplomatically with my perspective which I knew was in the minority. I hid my knowledge, though, a bad habit

I had learned while growing up to dumb myself down in the classroom. I learned that girls who raised their hand too often were found to be irritating. Boys liked the demure girls better. I have never been a demure female, but I learned to mimic my modest, quiet classroom sisters, and in doing so, began to unwittingly train myself to dumb down my knowledge. It seemed more girly to me to do so and God knows that even at such a young age I was working hard to fit in. Thus, a terrible habit had been ingrained into the fabric of my being and intellect. Now as a thirty-something year old woman, I had learned to deny my intelligence in order to appear more feminine, even at a woman's Bible study.

I loved studying. One year for Christmas my husband gave me Bible study software. Other women wanted jewelry and perfume under the Christmas tree; I longed for a multi-disc Bible study software suite of Bible commentaries and reference books. I accessed it often during the women's Bible study as well as my book collection which included several titles that tackled the issue of women and what the Bible *really meant*. But it was an uphill battle.

"If God doesn't want women to lead over men then what can we say about Deborah the Judge in the Old Testament or Priscilla whom Paul respected in the New Testament, or Miriam the Prophetess, sister of Moses who had spiritual leadership in Israel?" I asked one week.

One woman challenged my thought saying, "People always use those verses to try and squirm their way out of submission!"

A slight burn of anger rose up within me. "Stay low. Stay humble," I chanted within as I did my best to maintain a poker face. The tightrope of diplomacy is always maintained with tension.

Sometimes the discussions become vulnerable. This was revealing in how deeply women were affected by teachings from the church. "I feel like a doormat sometimes," said one young mother who began to cry as she let out that admission.

"I know I'm wrong, but sometimes I feel as if the church and God treat women like doormats."

Other women around the room nodded in sympathy. The pain of the doctrine of submission lied there in the middle of our circle as we sat with Bibles on our laps. What could have become a powerful time of storytelling, of confessions of angst and misgivings with our Christian faith, instead remained paralyzed in the grip of traditionalism and silence.

She cried, but tears were brushed away quickly, composure regained and onward we went, putting the moment behind us as we carried on with learning that the Bible requires us to submit. "We don't really understand submission," said our Bible study leader, "or we'd be doing it. I'm going to ask my husband to teach on this sometime."

Inwardly I groaned while other women sat quietly for that is what we do. We stay hidden behind the walls of what my friend Jim Henderson calls *beliefism*[84] the devotion to a system of beliefs no matter the cost. It's about being right and keeping others right. Beliefism sucks the life out of independent thought. Beliefism is being spoon-fed what to think and believe and to be suspicious of others who believe differently.

It intimidates women to maintain the party line, to keep in rank so as not to cause a fuss. A friend of mine says she was anxious about causing division when she realized that the rampant misogyny at her church was eating away at her soul. She quietly exited without saying out loud how devalued she had felt as a woman and particularly as a woman leader. Beliefism does that. It stifles women into a different kind of submission, into a submission of silence.

There were several moments throughout the two-month study that I was allowed to say my piece. I'd quote Galatians 3:28 about there being no male or female as we are all one in Christ; I'd point out the examples of women in authority throughout scripture, and I wondered out loud in my most diplomatic tone (of course) if perhaps women really were made in the image of God just the same as men. "What if we are meant to serve and lead alongside one another?" I asked. "What if submission is meant to be mutual rather than singular?"

My questions floated around the room like bubbles blown from a child's bubble wand. They weren't grappled with or given much attention. They hung there for a moment, suspended by the weightlessness of indifference. And then, we'd move on to the next thing, putting behind us the ideas of equality between the sexes, which evaporated into the oblivion of beliefism. There was no reflective discourse. No examining of another way of looking at women's roles from a different biblical viewpoint. This study became a highlighted entry to me of a lifetime of being told what to believe and think. There was no spirit of inquiry, no indication of a willingness to see or at least get a glimpse of a different point of view.

This lack of interest to dialog about other possibilities of what the scriptures teach is partly rooted in the way women are taught. The teaching method in most churches is parishioners passively listen while Bible teachers—usually men—deposit their vast Bible knowledge like currency into hearts and minds. This kind of teaching method is known as a "banking education."[85]

Paulo Freire, the person who developed the banking concept and who is considered to be one of the most innovative influential educators of the 20th century, writes this:

> In the banking concept of education, knowledge is
> a gift bestowed by those who consider themselves
> knowledgeable upon those whom they consider to know
> nothing.[86]

This has been my experience in most of my church life. Bible teachers deposit into us doctrines and creeds with the expectation that the uneducated nod and agree. Thus, women are told what to believe about ourselves—be submissive—with little room to discover other ideas unless we pursue them on our own. Little wonder when a horde of Bible preachers tell women over and over again that God has designed her to submit to the men he designed to rule.

It would have been remarkable if this Bible study had addressed the tension and distress of the doctrine of submission with critical thinking instead of groupthink.

Freire says that banking education "anesthetizes and inhibits creative power."[87] I am convinced that women throughout Christendom accept our role as lesser than because not only is that what we are taught to know, but we are also taught not to question. Creative thinking is repressed, not with deliberateness, but as a result of Christ followers trusting the pastor and his sermon Sunday after Sunday.

Freire also notes that banking education "resists dialog."[88] This was missing from the Bible study like most other Bible studies I've attended over the last thirty years. A good dose of dialog would have given women in that room the opportunity to think beyond the boundaries of their traditionalistic perspective.

Beliefism cannot thrive in an atmosphere of dialog. Dialog could have been a catalyst for some of those women in discovering that they are not doormats in God's eyes, but human beings made in the fullness of God's image.

I think this is a big reason why my women's listening parties continue to thrive. Dialog is the centerpiece of our gatherings. The spirit of inquiry my friend Deborah Loyd teaches about is honored and welcomed. Women are free to voice doubts and ask hard questions, to speak of experiences and feelings that seem to defy scripture and God himself. It is liberating.

When the study was over, I gave the Bible study leader a copy of Loren Cunningham and David Hamilton's book, *Why Not Women?* This is a great book that features some of the best biblical scholarship on women in leadership in an easy-to-read-narrative. I told her, "If you read it I'll take you out to lunch and then we can talk about it. I'd love to hear your thoughts." I was truly hoping for at least a private dialog between the two of us on the issues raised in the study.

She never called, but one Sunday at church, not too long later, she handed me a photocopied sheaf of papers titled, *Biblical Manhood and*

Womanhood. I would later find out that these were a concise version of Piper and Grudem's book, *Recovering Biblical Manhood and Womanhood: A Response to Evangelical Feminism.*

"Read this. As an evangelical feminist this is something you need to read," she said.

I wasn't sure how I felt being labeled an evangelical feminist by a conservative Christian woman, but I did read it and if she was hoping it would convert me, it did not. In fact, the message of submission and female subservience is so strong in these writings that it served to only solidify my position that women are fully equal with men and made in the image of God.

She and I both proved to be strong-minded women with polarizing views about women and submission. And though our differences could have become volatile during the study, they did not. We both conducted ourselves with respect for one another's position, and I remained diplomatic I order to avoid conflict. Though to this day, I wish the group had evolved into a women's listening party of honest dialog and storytelling.

Over the next few weeks and months, several different women who had been a part of that study privately approached me. "Thank you so much for standing up to her," said one quiet spoken woman referring to our Bible study leader. "I'm scared to speak up, but I agreed with everything that you said." She had cornered me downstairs after church when we both were on our way to fetch our children from Sunday school.

"I wasn't trying to stand up to anyone," I said, "I just wanted to voice my point of view and let women know there's another way to look at things about women and leadership." A hidden spring of anxiety bubbled up from somewhere within. I was not looking to be a rebel rouser.

"Well, I'm glad you were there. I could never have said the things that you did," she continued. By now she had leaned close in to me, practically whispering in my ear her misgivings with the takeaway message of the study: women mind your place as the subservient gender. "I don't think the Bible really teaches that, but I don't know how to say it or that I'll get it wrong," she confided. "I'm just glad somebody like you was there to speak up."

Another woman soon approached me with similar misgivings. She was a medical student nearing the finish of her studies. "I was so glad you spoke up the way you did," she said one Sunday morning after service when no one else was around. "I can't believe Christian women in this day and age still think they have to walk behind their men like servants," she said. "I think the people of this church are great, but they have got to join the 20th century."

Our conversation was brief. I barely knew her, but I wondered later why she had not spoken a single word about her conviction for women and equality during the two-month long Bible study?

Other women also spoke to me of their confusion about what the Bible says about women. "I went to that study hoping to learn that women are valued the same as men, but instead I left it early. I don't want to stop following Christ over this, but it seems like God is against women as if we're second-class citizens in his kingdom," confided a married woman who I knew had been a part of the congregation for many years. Her admission stunned me as well as concerned me.

How many other women in our church felt the way these women did? Who else quietly supported the equality of women and men in all areas of church life and leadership? Worse, who else was dying on the inside, their faith in God under threat?

I was beginning to realize that there was an invisible, secret society of free thinkers roaming the church without hall passes. And though I had spoken up during the study with the lightest voice that I could manage, it had become like a pebble dropped into a pond with gentle ripples spreading across the water.

The still waters of a women's theology in my church had been stirred, barely, but definitely stirred. In the years to come, I would discover that many Christian women desire a deeper theology for themselves beyond the beliefism of submission, but they remain quiet, as if literally fulfilling the words Paul wrote to Timothy, "Let a woman learn in silence ..."

Sue Monk Kidd says that, "Silence becomes the female drug of choice."[89] Women of faith have become dependent on silence. It is overdue for the daughters of the church to detox and discover the power of creative questioning and speaking up in a spirit of inquiry and even dissent.

~~

I had gladly allowed a stained glass ceiling to be built inside of me in my formation years as a Christ follower. I thought it was the true path for a Christian woman. The only path.

For a lot of years, I was like most of the women at that Bible study. It was like encountering a previous version of myself. I used to defend the submission of women, too, defending it to the bone as God's holy will. But after strong dialog with my friend Tracey in Hong Kong, my point of view broadened. I began to explore books and studies that presented biblical teaching supporting the equality of women with men. But I kept much of my new found knowledge to myself.

After a few years had rolled past and by the time I had landed in that women's Bible study, I had developed a firm code of diplomacy: I would not be divisive about the issue of women and church which I viewed solely as a theological issue and nothing else.

But in my quest to avoid being divisive, I chose to sedate myself with silence, rarely speaking up for women under any circumstance. Which is what made my participation in the women's Bible study all the more extraordinary!

Though my inner stained glass ceiling developed large cracks that I can track back to Tracey, it was still, after all, a filter on my mind. I still accepted with a great deal of tacit acceptance, that the inequality of women in church was just a doctrinal dispute, an irritating reality that I had to make the best of.

But my inner stained glass filter took a big hit in the pivotal conversation with Rose Swetman in Seattle. "The issue of women in the church is not an issue of theology, but an issue of justice," she had said. Those words still echo in my mind these several years later. That was the point when my stained glass filter began to crack open wide until finally, it exploded. I had realized that the equality of women with men is an issue of justice. Not a doctrinal position.

After that, I became more aware of the prevalence of Christianized sexism towards women in the church, especially on the Internet. With the explosion of digital communication, the obstacle of stained glass ceiling thinking has become more visible. I had not noticed it before, the stained glass inside of me effectively filtering much of it out of my conscious awareness. But now I had new eyes. I had experienced an awakening.

At one point, I came across some online articles that warned of the church becoming *feminized* and the need for men to *man up*. Instead of ignoring it, as I would have in my former diplomatic self, I blogged about it. And in blogging about it, I was learning to find my voice and my power in resisting the injustice of inequality towards women, even the polite forms of oppression that appear in the digital spaces of blog rants and emails.

So when someone in my circle of email contacts forwarded me a rather demeaning devotion towards women, I could not just ignore it and delete it. I was on a mission.

The writer had cited Genesis 3, about Eve and the scandalous fruit incident, to caution her readers that women are weaker than men. With my new eyes I perceived this slighting of women as more than a doctrinal view. I now saw it as unfair and detrimental to the collective sisterhood of women everywhere. I was tempted to delete it until I read her closing statements where she reminded her readers to remember that because of Eve, women are more vulnerable to spiritual manipulation and deception. I couldn't let that go. So, I hit reply. Or more accurately, I hit Reply All.

The emailer had sent the devotional to dozens of her friends in her enthusiasm to remind us of the special burden we carry as the "weaker sex." I decided to email this group my misgivings about the message of the devotional. I wrote:

> Women are made in the image of God as much as men are. To say that women are the weaker sex is to say that there is a lesser side of God that is also prone to deception and vulnerable to manipulation. I disagree. Women possess the same qualities of discernment and intelligence that our brothers do. The story of Adam and Eve in the garden illustrates humankind's interdependence upon one another—not the inferiority of one sex beneath another.

The emailer, someone whom I barely knew but somehow had an email connection to, responded to my Reply All email with the defensive statement, "I was only trying to encourage women." I was annoyed by her response. Sending a message that advises me to guard my thinking since I'm the weaker sex doesn't exactly push my encouragement button.

A few other women on the email list wrote to me with notes of gratitude for speaking up. I had barely scratched the surface. It wasn't like I'd written a scathing editorial to a big city newspaper, but certainly it was something I would not have done in my previous diplomatic self.

It was an email, a simple email that I wrote in less than five minutes. Yet it accomplished something significant for me, a new beginning in actively resisting the oppression of women in the church, even polite forms of oppression like emails. It was the beginning of my liberation from censoring myself for so many years.

It also became another new point of consciousness for me. From there, I began to realize that even in mundane transactions of ordinary life the inequity of women in Christianity is normalized and unquestioned. So much so that a devotion such as this was genuinely meant to offer encouragement for other women. It was a vivid demonstration to me that women of faith have become incredibly domesticated to accept our oppression as *lesser than* as a form of spiritual piety.

Breaking silence about my views of women as equals with men revealed that something inside of me had broken, those panes of the stained glass ceiling that had distorted my vision of women and of myself. I had no idea that in hiding my true self I had also hidden my true voice. Once that inner obstacle was removed, I began to flourish in new ways as my true self and true beliefs became unfettered. My previous fears of being divisive if I was outspoken began to unravel, and as they did, my voice became louder and clearer.

I began to blog frequently on the topic of women's equality in the church, a topic which always provoked a flurry of comments and criticisms. But as I spoke up, and kept speaking up, I was discovering a new company of women who were just like me: Women who are determined to live in the fullness of who God has made them to be rather than diminished by what patriarchal religion tells them they cannot be.

~~

Every spring at a rustic resort on the outskirts of Portland, dozens of Christian women come together for a unique gathering known simply as Convergence.[90] Each year is filled with conversation and guided group activities to help us unfurl the longings within that tend to remain unspoken. It's not your typical women's retreat. Instead of having a keynote speaker, attendees themselves speak into each other's lives through a series of group interactions and activities.

One of my favorite things about this annual conference are the spontaneous break-out group sessions that spring up. Women volunteer to lead on whatever topic is of interest to them and participants then choose which session to join. One year I organized a talk around the notion of unladylike Christian women.

We met up at the Power Station, one of the restaurants located at the resort. I didn't realize until later how appropriate (and prophetic) the name of our meeting spot was.

About six women joined me and over hot cups of tea and coffee, we discussed how the church has shaped and informed our identity as women. One young woman shared at length how her ultra conservative upbringing had confused her about marriage. "All I had ever seen was submission by all the women in my family and in my church," she said.

Other women talked about how their sense of womanhood had become bruised when they failed to become the ideal Christian woman. We talked and listened to each other, allowing the discussion to flow where it would as women are so fond of doing. It was a great listening party. This is probably why I enjoy the spontaneity of these break-out sessions so much – it results in a burst of listening parties all over the grounds of the resort.

Last spring we did something new at Convergence. It was a powerful group activity to help us outwardly express what was inwardly happening in our lives. It was like a communal art project.

Shards of stained glass were stacked on a large table. A hammer was provided and also plastic kitchen storage bags. Each woman placed a piece of stained glass in a bag and smashed it with the hammer, the shard fragmenting into dozens of colorful pieces as tiny as pocket change. We then took our slivered shards and glued them together onto a large window that had been erected for the activity. The little broken pieces created a beautiful mosaic swirling with reds, blues, yellows and other colors. As each woman took her turn, the mosaic grew in width and length.

When it came to my turn, I spontaneously grabbed a sharpie and wrote the word IDENTITY on my piece of glass. As I placed it in the bag and raised the hammer to it, I pictured myself in all of my womanly glory floating up to the church rafters, my fingers reaching out to caress the stained glass ceiling. That's what I did for so many years, I touched it, polished it, and kept it looking saintly and sacred. I tamed the feminine image of God within me to stay in the shadows, to stay quiet and diplomatic.

I raised the hammer and smashed the glass, my word IDENTITY breaking into dozens of scattered bits. The letters became undecipherable, just like my former polite, ladylike self. I carefully removed the pieces, adding them to the collective mosaic of Convergence women. A new society of women birthed before my eyes, a sisterhood of shattered stained glass and identities. I felt a ripple in the spirit realm, as if the powers of darkness shuddered for this is the kind of spiritual freedom the devil fears.

We did this quietly, reverently. For me, it was a public act of declaring my break with the past of a hierarchic-informed identity as a woman of God. I reveled within, elbow to elbow with women like me who embraced the whole image of God in our female selves. It was a collective rebellion against the lie that Women are less.

~~

Women aren't the only ones throwing rocks and taking hammers to religious obstacles. A group known as The Elders[91] have taken to throwing rocks at stained glass ceilings, too. This is an independent group of eminent global leaders brought together by South Africa's Nelson Mandela. Members of this group include Desmond Tutu, Kafin Anan, Aung San Suu Kye, as well as former President Jimmy Carter. The group's mission is "to offer their collective influence and experience to support peace building, help address major causes of human suffering and promote the shared interests of humanity."[92]

The list of areas of human suffering they have devoted themselves to alleviating includes reconciliatory forums for nations in turmoil such as Cypress and Myanmar (formerly known as Burma), the dismantling of nuclear weapons and also the advancement for equality for women and girls. I found it telling that they begin their pleas for gender equality by first appealing to the religious traditions of the world where women experience religious-driven oppression and inequity. They write:

> We believe that women and girls share equal rights with
> men and boys in all aspects of life. We call upon all

leaders to promote and protect equal rights for women and girls. We especially call on religious and traditional leaders to set an example and change all discriminatory practices within their own religions and traditions. (The Elders, July 2, 2009)[93]

There is a vast continuum of all sorts of oppression and human suffering around the world. It is significant to me that this A-list of world leaders who have triaged their concerns for the planet have included not only injustices committed against women and girls, but specifically against religious-inspired injustice.

In a speech former President Jimmy Carter gave at a meeting of the Parliament of the World's Religions, he said:

My own Southern Baptist Convention leaders ordained in recent years that women must be "subservient" to their husbands and prohibited from serving as deacons, pastors, chaplains in the military service, or teachers of men. They based this on a few carefully selected quotations from Saint Paul and also Genesis, claiming that Eve was created second to Adam and was responsible for original sin. This was in conflict with my belief that we are all equal in the eyes of God. [94]

Reading sites like The Elders fans the flame within me that I am a not a crazy woman who needs to get over herself. The reason I allowed myself to be inhibited by a pretty stained glass ceiling for so long was because I thought it was just me. *It's me. I'm the wounded one who needs to understand my feminine role in the kingdom of God and humanity. I'm the one with issues. It's all Me.*

And this is the insidious nature of the polite oppression of women in churches and faith tribes across many denominations. We blame ourselves. We discount our own intuition and critical thinking skills for we have been told over and over again that we cannot be trusted to think for ourselves.

I once prayed with a young woman who had secretly felt a deep call to the pastorate, but she had no mental framework to accommodate such a desire. People she loved and respected had taught her that girls do not grow up to be pastors. Not with overt sermons in her moderate church, but by the nature of the face of her church—exclusive male leadership and Bible teaching her entire life that exalted male power, as well as the glaring omission of women teaching from the Sunday pulpit—these were the unspoken yet powerful messages she soaked into her little girl heart over and over again, so that by the time adolescence came and with it the inspiration to teach and preach, she had nowhere to go with her sense of calling, except the rails of shame and guilt for having such a desire.

The polite oppression of her identity as female was a velvet-lined cell that offered her comfort if she remained in the status quo of traditionalism. What she did not know was that liberation into her full humanity and feminine power was not anti-biblical nor anti-God, and not even anti-church or anti-man. No, the only thing it threatened was anti-traditionalism for without a doubt the force of a woman's willing subservience in the world of church is her commitment to uphold the system of tradition that put her there in the first place.

Women have been taught to be complicit in our own oppression in the church. We need a movement of women and men to teach us how to resist these messages of inequality and to occupy our space of full personhood together. The church needs transformation in how half its members are esteemed and treated. If not now, then when? If not us, then who?

Chapter Nine: Resisting Resignation

Women are the change

> The only tired I was, was tired of giving in.
>
> Rosa Parks, Civil Rights activist

> I do not wish [women] to have power over men; but over themselves.[95]
>
> Mary Wollstonecraft, 16th century author

> But the history of the world shows the vast majority, in every generation, passively accept the conditions into which they were born, while those who demand larger liberties are ever a small, ostracized minority, whose claims are ridiculed or ignored.
>
> Elizabeth Cady Stanton, 19th century abolitionist and women's rights activist

"**W**e're not waiting for permission anymore," said Deborah to the group of women crowded together in my living room for our monthly women's listening party. "Women can create our own paradigms, our own stories and experiences. We don't need to wait for anyone to give us permission to do or be what God has meant for us."

Heads nodded in unison as she spoke, the group ranging in age and experience, yet each one holding in common the oppression of inequality. "It means we have to get creative," continued Deborah, her dreadlocks swaying as she turned her head to see each woman around the room. "We get to be in charge of what we want our story to look like."

Deborah is one who speaks from experience. She overcame gender inequality when she made the bold decision to enroll at a seminary in pastoral studies that was not supportive of women being pastors.

"Why did you do that?" I asked her at one of our frequent coffee meet-ups.

"Because I wanted to learn how to defend women and how to teach this to my community," she replied. "What better place than a seminary? And they were happy to have me. They didn't agree with me being a pastor, but they welcomed me as a student and I learned a lot."

The women in my living room hung on to every word Deborah said, as they always do when she speaks. She has an extraordinary gift of teaching and is one of the most relatable theologians I know.

"To be an empowered woman means I don't have to resist," said Deborah. "I'm not going to let the system define me. I won't stay in it."

The system she was referring to is the system of patriarchal Christianity that keeps its women marginalized in subservient roles. The room lit up as we talked this over, this idea that resistance to inequality in the church is an upstream exercise of futility.

"Is it?" I wondered out loud. "Does that mean women ought to exit the system if she feels oppressed?" It seemed to me that the very act of leaving a church or faith tradition because of inequality was not only an action of protest, but a statement of resistance, of no longer enduring the oppression of women.

"Well, I want to slay my own dragons with the power of God," answered my friend Raseny, a young Southeast Asian American who has felt the brunt of inequality from two cultures her entire life—that of her conservative Asian ancestry and also from her conservative family of faith. "I want to be open to all that God has for me and not have someone else tell me what I can't do or can't be. I am resisting those lies and won't be held back waiting for someone to validate my equality with men."

"I can't stay in the system anymore," said another woman who was new to my listening party. "That's why I had to leave my last church. I loved this church, they do so much good, but I could no longer ignore the way women are treated as less than." Her voice cracked with emotion as hidden pain was uncovered. The feminine wound came out into the light in the room of her sisters. We shared that moment with her. We held her with our attentiveness, honoring the self-discovery she was on.

This is why I love my listening parties so much. In having a space with other women who will listen to our stories, we bring our pain into the open where I believe we experience release and healing. The power of community and of listening is an effective means of recovery and transformation. For many, I think, it's also an act of resistance in speaking out to a lifetime of messages that woman is less than.

"My husband and I also made a decision to leave a really good church," said Emily, a new friend whom I had met at a Christians for Biblical Equality conference in nearby Seattle. "The church we were a part of is active in social justice issues, but my husband said that the unjust way they view and treat women ... " Her voice also broke as strong emotion found its way to the surface. "I'm sorry. I knew I'd be crying before the night is over."

We all smiled. Some of us cried with her. I don't know what it is about tears, but they are contagious, and so much more cathartic when wept in the company of other women. "The way this church views and treats women causes more injustice than all the good they are trying to do in their social justice ministries," she continued. A collective groan of sympathetic resonance emitted from the group. It was true, I realized, startled at the irony of it all.

I have heard many stories and seen many tears shed over the injustice of inequality towards women in the body of Christ. It cripples women. It is not about a doctrine or divine God's created order. These are smokescreens, diabolical distractions that keep the focus off the oppressed who are walking wounded. Countless numbers of women suffer quietly in the halls of their churches, confused if their sense of second-class citizenship is real or imagined. And even if it's determined to be real, throngs of women resolve to just make the best of it rather than make a fuss. They don't want to smudge the stained glass ceiling.

Jim Henderson has written a book about this called *The Resignation of Eve: What if Adam's Rib is No Longer Willing to be the Church's Backbone?*[96] This book is a collection of vignettes that Jim collected as he examined the American church landscape by listening to women to discover their experiences and points of view. He interviewed many women who have responded in a variety of ways to the injustice of inequality.

Some of the stories he collected are from women who are resigned to accepting the oppression of inequality as inevitable. It was this group that concerned me the most, women who've given up dreaming of a different future for their daughters.

I believe it is this spirit of resignation that keeps women complicit in our own oppression. It is a spirit of hopelessness and helplessness that must be resisted if we are to experience true equality and mutual submission throughout the kingdom of God.

~~

When I lived in Hong Kong I taught English to Vietnamese refugees. Thousands of Vietnamese refugees poured out of their country after 1975 when South Viet Nam fell to Communist forces. Many fled on small boats across the South China Sea to the (then) British colony of Hong Kong in hopes of finding refuge. I heard many firsthand accounts of Communist oppression.

One young man told me that though it had been more than twenty years since the fall of Saigon, his family still suffered discrimination since his father had been an officer in the South Vietnamese army. "I left my country, everything that I know for freedom," he said, his dark brown eyes brimming with a lifetime of love and pain. "I did not want my family to grow up under Communism."

He saved his money to buy passage on a small boat for himself, his wife and their young son. Miraculously, everyone on their tiny boat survived even through a squall that nearly capsized their boat. "I risked it all for freedom," he said.

Those words hung between us like a flag declaring allegiance. My heart swelled with a mixture of sorrow and admiration for the man before me. He was more than a refugee. He was a reformer in the lineage of his family, a true history changer who was forever altering the storyline of his future ancestors.

Earlier this year (2011) began a groundswell of revolutions around the Arab world. Millions of citizens in Tunisia, Egypt and Yemen rose up in revolt against the oppressive governments of their nations. Rampant civil disobedience and widespread resistance resulted in deeply rooted systems being challenged or even toppled by the sheer will and anger of the people. I watched it on television, read about it on Twitter and Facebook as people on the other side of the world determined to change their nation and change their story.

In the 19th century, a writer named Harriet Beecher Stowe[97] wrote a book titled, *Uncle Tom's Cabin*, a fictionalized account of the brutal life and death of an American slave. A devout abolitionist, Harriet participated in the anti-slavery movement with the best weapon she had: her pen. She and her family had never owned slaves, but the stories she heard of the beatings and inhumane treatment of her black brothers and sisters moved her to write the novel which famed Russian writer Leo Tolstoy proclaimed as being "the highest moral art." [98]

Many considered her book, which sold millions of copies, as being the first shot of the American Civil War. Legend says that when President Abraham Lincoln met Harriet he said to her, "So you are the little woman that wrote the book that started this Great War?"

A Vietnamese refugee, revolutionary Arab citizens, and a 19th century abolitionist writer don't initially seem to hold a lot in common. But they do. They all refused to resign themselves to oppression and injustice. Whether by fleeing, revolting or speaking out, these were people who confronted the conditions of an unjust system in the way they saw fit in their context. They did not negotiate nor settle for diplomatic gestures and they definitely did not resign themselves to fatalistic acceptance.

"Resignation only leads to indifference,"[99] says Holocaust survivor, Elie Wiesel. Resignation is a kind of pain medication that keeps a person inactive, as if bound in a hospital bed with an I.V. drip keeping them sedated.

Women of faith who realize the demise of inequality must not give themselves over to resignation. We need some of the fire that burned inside Thelma from the 1991 film, *Thelma and Louise*, who said, "I've had it up to my ass with sedate."

There is a generation coming up behind us who are wondering what legacy we shall leave them with. We must not acquiescence to the oppression of women in the church for their sake as well as our own.

The choices I make today as a woman of faith are not just choices about the here and now, but strung together they become an heirloom pearl necklace that's passed onto the next generation of women and men. We have inherited our own pearls from the great strides in women's equality because of the women and men who came before us. This is because they did not yield to resignation. For example, we have our ancestors to thank that women have a voice to vote, a right that was not granted American women until 1920. Our grandmothers and great-grandmothers fought for that right. They were the brave women before us who would settle for nothing less and who certainly did not resign themselves to making the best of the way things were.

Thinking about my daughter is a part of my own story in resisting resignation. As my husband and I struggled through a decision of whether or not to remain in a church we were a part of, I began to evaluate the pros and cons. We had both come to a place of disillusionment with institutional Christianity. As I considered the spiritual scene we were a part of, I had to face this fact: in keeping myself in a suffocating environment that wounded its women, I was teaching my daughter how to do the same.

Oppression is generational. We teach it to the next generation and on it goes. But like the Vietnamese refugee who was motivated by his son's future, I realized I had to get her out. I had to exit the forms of my religion that treated women as less than not only for myself, but for my daughter and even for my son. I had to leave a system that not only perpetuated inequality but also defended it in the name of God. I could no longer reconcile myself with such a system no matter how many good feelings were snarled up inside of me.

Writer Susan Campbell articulates in her book, *Dating Jesus: A Story of Fundamentalism, Feminism and the American Girl,* how her own dance between resistance and resignation began in her girlhood as she keenly observed the unspoken coding of girls as the submissive gender:

> After being quarantined in the nursery with the babies, I am growing less comfortable with the compromises I've made in my head. I love Jesus, but if all believers are urged to stay the straight and narrow, there seems to be an especially narrow road built for women. I do not know how to talk about this. I can't ask my mother. I sense she doesn't chafe nearly as much as I do under what are starting to look like very clear restrictions. She has tried to teach me how to get what I want from men—by flattery and subterfuge, mostly—but I haven't the patience for diplomacy and it annoys me that I must go through men to get what I want in the first place. Saying this all out loud will label me in some way I can't yet define. And so I keep quiet.[100]

She may have kept quiet in her youth, but in her book Susan tells of the disconcerted messages she waded through in discovering who she was as well as who the real Jesus was. Telling the true confessions of what our experiences as females in the world of church has been like is a necessary rite of passage in order to own our story and then to change it.

Being overly polite about the story we find ourselves in won't do us much good. Sometimes we have to kick up a storm, make a fuss if only within earshot to whoever will pay attention to our protest. For Christian women who have been domesticated to regard as sinful behavior anything that resembles "getting ugly," it can be a form of resistance in the telling.

I love what civil rights activist Florynce Kennedy said:

> You've got to rattle your cage door. You've got to let them
> know that you're in there, and that you want out. Make
> noise. Cause trouble. You may not win right away, but
> you'll sure have a lot more fun.[101]

We need to be outspoken. We need to inoculate ourselves against resignation. We need our heralds, our prophets and activists, our poets and storytellers and preachers and teachers to speak the unmentionables, to express in the light of the day that which is kept hidden in the dark corners of the basement. For in the heralding we inspire one another to herald our selves, to prophesy to the dead bones that reside within until they wake up and dance.

That's what my friend Tracey did all those years ago in Hong Kong when she debated me about the biblical equality of women to teach and preach. Rose Swetman was also a prophetic beacon for me in my wilderness as a woman of faith.

My listening parties have evolved into a wayfarer's station of encouragement and information for women. We don't just show each other our scars from the injustice of inequality; we also inspire one another to be thoroughly human. Our gender was never intended to hold us back. Women carry the full image of God as much as men do. I cannot accept, and I do not think the Bible teaches, that God created women in subservient roles. I don't think that's a true story.

All through writing this book—which for me has been my greatest act of resistance to patriarchal Christianity—I have leaned hard into listening to these women at my listening parties. I listen to them unravel the web of fables that have informed and shaped their womanhood. Their honesty, their disclosure of their pain and struggles has enriched me in so many ways. It resembles in some ways a recovery group as we tell each other the myths that have marred us, but also the true stories of our true selves. This takes courage.

In her extraordinary teaching DVD, *The Hustle for Worthiness*,[102] Dr. Brene Brown says that owning our story is the bravest thing we'll ever do. "Our sense of worthiness resides inside our story," she says.

Women of faith must resolve to own our story. It doesn't belong to anyone else. In owning our story, we gain courage in being heard and received for who we are and how we are. We can't expect others to respect our power if we don't believe we have any. Whether rough and rowdy or with quiet, steely meekness, women need to tear off the veil of resignation and be seen and heard for who we are.

Writer Mary Wilson Little says, "Politeness is half good manners and half good lying." It is overdue for Christ-following women to let go of ladylike propriety and all the lies that come with it.

When I lived in Hong Kong I became acquainted with Jackie Pullinger, a missionary from England who had established near-legend status by the time I had arrived in the mid eighties. Jackie felt called to be a missionary from a young age. By the time she reached young adulthood, she was ready to go out into the world. But it was the sixties. None of the missionary societies at that time would send a young, unmarried woman.

A wise, spiritual leader advised her to follow God's lead and just go. So with a few dollars in her pocket and a one-way ticket around the world on a ship, Jackie headed into her adventure of faith. She landed in the busy port of Hong Kong and felt that God wanted her there.

In her book, *Chasing the Dragon*,[103] Jackie tells the stories of how she ended up in Hong Kong's infamous Walled City, an area rife with drugs, crime and gang violence. Many were afraid to venture anywhere near the Walled City, but empowered by God's Spirit of love, Jackie penetrated one of the darkest strongholds of Southeast Asia at that time. She was, and remains, one of the heroines of the faith.

Despite Jackie's ministry accomplishments, she still had to overcome the obstacles that were put in front of her by those who could not see her gifting, but only her gender. Of her critics she said:

> Isn't it wonderful that God would choose a woman to go? I would say, "No, it's not wonderful." Excuse me for being rude about God, but he can pick who he likes. I mean, it's no more wonderful for him to send a woman than a man, or an old man or young woman. He picks who he wants. That's his business. It was God's wisdom that sent me. I was just doing what he made me for. That's no credit to me; it's all credit to him. If he's made you for something, you just do it.[104]

I love her attitude. God can pick who he likes. And he does. The Creator is not restrained by social and cultural conditioning or patriarchal worldviews like we are. God is an equal opportunity Leader.

Christ followers need a transformation in our thinking. We need to live and act by the conviction that all are created in the full image of God. That gifting is a matter of calling, not gender. The issue of women and equality is not merely an issue of theology, but an urgent issue of justice. We need to live and act like we believe this.

It pains me that my sisters of the faith who know these things and yet continue to serve a system of Christianized sexism, have become complicit in their own oppression. I say this because for many years that was me. I was the one aiding the polite oppression of women every time I submitted myself to silence. I may have been noble in my attitude wanting to avoid being divisive, but I blindly divided my voice and myself. This is not becoming of a spirit of reconciliation, but furthers the disunion of women with men.

Resignation paralyzes women from reexamining ourselves and our stories from a new narrative. When patriarchy is the narrator, even the Bible becomes a character in keeping us marginalized. We have no spunk or fire to imagine anything different. And so, the story goes unchallenged and unchanged.

Freire writes, "Resignation gives way to the drive for transformation and inquiry."[105] A spirit of resignation drains a woman of healthy questioning and evaluating. Her mind mistakes the crumbs of liberty for true and whole freedom. She protests when it's suggested that the unjust treatment of women thrives virtually unchallenged in the contemporary church. Resignation to inequality serves no one in the kingdom of God except the power system of patriarchy.

So what can a woman do? How can she resist resignation?

Just as each woman has a unique story that she must own for herself, so too, must each woman in her context determine how to oppose the injustice of inequality if it exists in her faith tribe. For some women it will mean making the excruciating decision to exit in order to live out their story. That's what my friends Mimi, Jodi and Deborah did. It cost all of them varying degrees of sacrifice, but none of them would ever go back to resigning themselves to an unjust faith system. They each found a new story to live out, a new paradigm where women express the fullness of the image of God they carry.

Mimi and her husband Steve landed at The Bridge, a post-modern congregation of mostly young people in Portland. Me and my family began attending The Bridge about the same time. Mimi and I have both experienced the beauty of equality at this faith community. There is no position paper to explain the leadership of women in the church. There have been no meetings to debate what the Bible says about women and spiritual authority, and there are no seminars for women to learn instruction in how to be godly, submissive wives. Men and women run elbow to elbow at The Bridge. The Spirit is utterly free to choose whom the Spirit would choose for any ministry. Women have as much voice as men. It is the only faith tribe I've ever been a part of where equality is a core value.

This value of inclusion was woven into the story of The Bridge from its inception. Deborah and her husband Ken planted The Bridge in the late nineties. They came from a megachurch background and had experienced the patriarchal system of church for years. They determined not to replicate it when they ventured out on their own. They succeeded.

After a decade or so of pastoring at The Bridge, Ken felt called to begin another church for Portland's homeless community, a passion of his that has made him somewhat of a celebrity on the streets of the city. But it was his call, not Deborah's. As Ken left The Bridge, Deborah remained as one of the pastors, co-pastoring with two others. I remember when they announced all of this one Sunday.

"Are Ken and I getting divorced?" she asked as they explained that Ken would be moving on but she would be staying. "Of course not! Ken is doing what God has called him to do, and I'm doing what I'm called to do. We're still very much married to one another."

In any other context, this kind of reassurance would be laughable. Imagine a married couple who owns a shop explaining this to their employees if one moves on to begin a new business. No one would question the marriage commitment.

But in the world of church, which has been marred by patriarchy, married couples are most often seen serving in pastoral roles together, not apart. Deborah knew this, which is why she addressed this in a public meeting. She knew that for many of us it would be a new experience to be in a church where a woman was pastoring without her husband at her side.

Several years later Deborah felt stirred herself to move on from The Bridge to pursue teaching in seminary. In her wake, and Ken's, The Bridge is being co-pastored by two women and one man, none of them married to each other. They shepherd because they are called to shepherd, and it has nothing to do with their sexual identity.

My friend Kathy Escobar pastors a similar church, The Refuge, in Denver, Colorado. The first time I met Kathy she was speaking at a workshop at a conference I was attending. She joked when she introduced her co-pastor, Karl Wheeler, saying, "We're married, but not to each other."

These are examples of women who created faith communities that support the full measure of collaboration between women and men. No patriarchy allowed.

But most women are not called to leadership. We go to church, we volunteer, we help out in whatever ways we can, and though we may not pastor, nor lead, we feel the injustice of being relegated as the second sex. Such as one friend of mine who attended a large church with her family, but remained at a distance from the core church life.

"I kept wondering, 'Am I hearing a message of man-up for men, but submit for women?' I wasn't sure." And so she kept going, she and her young family in attendance every Sunday. "But then it became so clear to me one week. The pastor talked about husbands leading their wives, and women needing to submit to their husband's authority. I realized it wasn't just me, that I wasn't being insecure for feeling like the lesser sex. The church was teaching me this."

She announced to her husband that he could do what he wanted, but she would no longer be joining him at this church. She told him this with respect and firmness, making clear that she would not subject herself to a community that assigns women secondary roles in marriage and in the kingdom of God. He agreed and together they are searching for a new faith community where women equality is a value rather than a debate. This is what resistance looked like to her. She shed being ladylike in favor of being a woman.

My friend Jodi says that when she was agonizing over whether or not to leave her church that it finally boiled down to a simple act of obedience. "I had to obey God," she says. "Staying in the church I loved meant I had to deny who I was and the gifting God put inside of me. Being obedient to my calling meant I had to leave my church."

When women like Jodi, Mimi and De[ ] parties, other women listen with rapt attentioi patriarchal forms of Christianity not only lib also their spirituality. Oppression of any kind makes me wonder if womanhood is born whe

Friere writes:

> ... through transforming action, peopie can create a new situation, one which makes possible the pursuit of a fuller humanity. But the struggle to be more fully human has already begun in the authentic struggle to transform the situation."[106]

In other words, those who are oppressed—even if that oppression is polite—must themselves find a new narrative for their lives that honors the full image of God they carry.

This means that resistance is necessary, whatever that may look like in a woman's life. It means that resignation will get us nowhere. A sense of resignation that things are the way things are keeps women immobile and unimaginative.

I love what my friend Al Doyle wrote in a comment for an online article I wrote called, *The God-hearted Sexist*:

> Women must be prepared to declare the old order, out of order. Think ahead to the great mosaic that will come from all the fragments of the shattered stained glass ceiling rearranged in a new pattern.[107]

That's what I'm talking about, a new pattern of doing life and church together, a vibrant display of men and women in collaborative unison. This is the kingdom of God.

PART THREE

UNLADYLIKE

We shall awaken from our dullness and rise vigorously toward justice.

Hildegard of Bingen, Benedictine Abbess

and Christian Mystic, 11th Century

Chapter Ten: The Heresy of Her

The myth of the good Christian woman

One is not born a woman, one becomes a woman.[108]

Simone de Beauvoir, French feminist writer

Well behaved women seldom make history.

Laurel Thatcher Ulrich, historian

I was driving along the Columbia River corridor on highway fourteen, headed towards Beacon Rock, a massive monolith that rises up from the river like a misplaced island. I navigated my minivan along the winding road. Green groves of old growth forest lined the highway like old men watching the changing times. I drove around a bend and as the tree line fell back an open meadow of emerald green grass welcomed me while a northwest breeze flirted with the trees. The mighty Columbia River rolled behind as the black ribbon of highway unraveled mile by mile.

I turned the radio on to keep me company as I drove. I rarely listen to Christian programs, but for some reason I tuned the dial to a popular Christian station, just in time for a broadcast from a well-known pastor. The velvety, smooth voice of the announcer introduced the topic of today's sermon: what the Bible says about women.

Ugh.

I could have switched the station and maybe I should have, but I wanted to hear it again, the traditionalist perspective of women and Bible interpretation. Having removed myself from patriarchal churches, I am no longer subject to messages about biblical womanhood. I'm a woman. I love the Bible. That's my version of biblical womanhood. But from time to time it's good for me to read articles or listen to radio broadcasts of those who hold fast to a complementarian viewpoint. It reminds me why I need to continue writing about the injustice of inequality.

"It's the spirit of this age and radical feminism," bellowed the preacher, "that has weak pastors refusing to tell the ladies in their congregations to follow the word of God instead of the world!"

I groaned, my heart begging me to change the station while my mind said, "No, listen and remember from whence you came."

"Radical feminism has infiltrated the church so that women are not fulfilling their God-given roles." His preach was beginning to sound more like a rant.

I cussed out loud at this point and reached for the knob to turn it off. I did not want my beautiful drive polluted with the rhetoric of oppression. But instead, I pulled my hand back to the steering wheel. I felt an inner nudge to listen to every word though I disagreed with what the preacher was saying.

"Women are insisting to be pastors and elders. In conforming to the world, Christian women who won't honor their God-given role as helpmates and homemakers are diminishing the gospel," said the preacher. "Instead of being led by the Spirit of the Lord, they are being led by the spirit of this age. So much in our culture allures women away from obeying the word."

The broadcast was divine timing for it added to the fire in my soul to keep writing and talking about these things, and to keep inviting women to listening parties in order to untangle the web of oppression together. Hearing the preacher insist that women are meant to remain home and serve their men in godly submission confirmed more than ever that I am meant to keep raising these issues as a writer and as a blogger.

I have no issue with women who choose to be homemakers, which is what I did for a few years when my kids were little, but to tell people of faith as this radio preacher did that women are *meant to stay home* is to opt women out of the liberty of self-determination. It also relegates women from public life and perpetuates a patriarchal worldview. Most of all, it teaches women to submit and quench their feminine power for the sake of Christian piety.

Patriarchal systems relegate men to public spaces and women to unseen spaces. It's the insistence that women are designed to be home managers and men are ordained to be church and civic managers. This one-dimensional view of gender roles limits women as well as men from the wide-open meadows of possibility.

"It is the business of the church to confront injustice," said my friend Kim at one of my listening parties. I think it's also our business to resist it, especially when it is within the household of faith. Women and men need to resist the myth that Christian women are destined to be submissive assistants.

In a commencement speech at Yale University, former President John F. Kennedy said, "The great enemy of the truth is very often not the lie, deliberate, contrived and dishonest, but the myth, persistent, persuasive and unrealistic."[109]

The myth of the good Christian woman is alive and well in the modern spheres of faith tribes and churches. We have bought into a myth. Many I've known over the years in my spiritual journey have been dedicated to transforming themselves into submissive women who please God, the church and their husbands if they are married.

Many years ago I was at a women's retreat of a conservative denomination I belonged to when living in California. I loved the women in this church and looked forward to a weekend getaway with them. The theme of the retreat was, "Being a Pleasing Woman to God." There was a speaker who told entertaining stories of her spiritual journey into becoming a mature woman of faith. She spoke a lot about laying down her rights in order to serve others. By weekend's end, several women were sharing that they needed to be more submissive in attitude and deed in order to please God. It became the prevailing message in nearly every testimony.

"I need to lay down my life more," said one woman. "I am too selfish," said another. "I have to put God and my family first instead of myself," asserted one middle-aged lady. One woman went so far as to tell us that she had decided during the weekend to quit her job, something her husband had wanted her to do for a long time in order for her to be home fulltime.

I appreciate the Christian discipline of self-denial, but when it comes to women of faith, we seem to tweak it to a different ideal of losing our self for the sake of who we imagine God wants us to be-the good Christian woman. She is our saint, our matron of all that is holy and approved of by God. She is the vision of true Christian womanhood: submissive, self-sacrificing, humble and domestic. She is what we have been taught to become.

This image of biblical womanhood appears to be a godly standard of femininity. But it is not. The good Christian woman is a semblance of a human being who does not entirely claim her humanity or otherwise we would imagine her with a host of other human characteristics such as leadership, strength, intellectual prowess, and so on. But instead, the good Christian woman is idealized with a few "feminine" qualities that are supposedly more sacred than other human qualities.

Dorothy Sayers writes about this with a switch of the sexes to make her point:

> Probably no man has ever troubled to imagine how strange his life would appear to himself if it were unrelentingly assessed in terms of his maleness; if everything he wore, said, or did had to be justified by reference to female approval if he were compelled to regard himself, day in

day out, not as a member of society, but merely as a virile member of society.[110]

Sayers makes the case that there are pressures upon women to live for the approval of men. This is patriarchy through and through when a woman's identity is shaped and judged by a male-centered worldview. To be a holy woman was and is to be a submissive woman. Thus, the ideal good Christian woman is a being—not a human being—but a spiritual being that has been invented by patristic thinkers.[111]

Patristic means pertaining to the early fathers of the Christian church or their writings. The patristic period of the church was during the church's formation when male church leaders and writers deepened patriarchal attitudes towards women by theologizing women as the lesser sex. John Chrysostom, a fifth century bishop of Constantinople, for example, said biblical women "were great characters, great women and admirable ... yet did they in no case outstrip the men, but occupied the second rank."[112]

There remains to this day a residue of this kind of sentiment towards women, even in the body of Christ, which is meant to express the presence of God in a dark and unjust world. It is from this well that the patriarchal view of women continues to be nourished. The church is desperately in need of the living water that Jesus offers a life force that renews the image of God within us rather than diminishes.

I maintain with all of my mind and heart that the notion of women as the second sex to men is not God's mandate. It does not come from his well. The good Christian woman is a myth.

~~

"Church taught me how to lie," says my friend and blogger Erin Word. We were sipping hot cups of coffee one afternoon while our children were in school. This was when Erin and I enjoyed a time span of being women of leisure, able to meet-up for womanly banter and dark brewed java. Those days are pretty much behind us, but the rich conversations we developed fueled by critical inquiry and caffeine have long stayed with me.

"I could not fill the role as a good Christian woman. It's a myth. She's a myth. And it was killing me," she said with eyes brimming with flashes of anger and triumph of liberty. Erin is a megachurch refugee. Part of her process in her departure from institutional Christianity has been sorting out who she is out from underneath the guise of the submissive Christian woman.

Erin and I have spent literally hundreds of hours processing our thoughts and experiences as Christ following women. We're both bloggers, we write and think out loud to sort out what we know and what we don't want to know anymore. Erin blogged often about her thoughts on trying to be a well-mannered ladylike woman of faith who followed the Bible:

> Some of you might call this process transformation, I call
> it oppression, for nothing in my heart of hearts was ever
> transformed; it was simply controlled and pressurized.
> When a woman is subjected to years of traditional
> teachings about submission and subservience, when she
> is taught how to dress, how to behave, how to talk, how
> to think ... which like it or not, this is what is happening
> in much of modern Christianity, even in progressive
> Christianity ... [113]

Pressurized is a good way to put it, and that even in some of our hip-looking ministry-savvy churches, women are still told to mind their place.

Together Erin and I tore down our houses of Christian misogyny board by board, helping each other dismantle the oppressive self-view the church had instilled in both of us. We were discovering a new way of looking at ourselves as we surveyed the rubble of our former submissive identities. At times, it felt as if something was vaporizing inside of us as our old roles as Christian women became deconstructed.

Our former pretty, submissive selves were on the verge of total collapse. Or rather, the roles we had tried so hard to fit into were collapsing. Like the fall of the Berlin Wall, the messaging that had bricked us in from expressing our true selves was becoming undone. We were becoming free.

Part of Erin's story is that in trying to conform to being a biblical model of a submissive woman, she not only nearly lost herself, but also her marriage.

"Where's the woman I married?" asked her husband when their relationship reached a crisis point. But as she abandoned trying to live up to the myth, she began to flourish in her personhood and as a result, her marriage was revitalized.

What was at stake was Erin's personal sovereignty and power of self-determination. The patriarchal concept of submission robs a woman of that. As Erin exited this story for her life, she came into a new view of herself and of her marriage. She began living out a new story, one of authenticity, of being her true self.

Brene Brown writes:

> Authenticity is something we revere in others and strive to maintain in our own lives. We don't feel good about half-truths, disingenuous connection and fearful silence … We tell people what they want to hear, or we don't speak out when we should. In turn, we feel shame for being dishonest, misrepresenting our beliefs, or not taking an important stand.[114]

Fearful silence, shame, misrepresentation, these are the fruits a woman bears when trying to be who she is not.

The injustice of inequality oppresses a woman to disengage from her authentic self. That's what happened to Erin, and that's what happened to me, as well as many of the women who've shared their innermost thoughts at my women's listening parties.

Being real is a battle. Letting go of the myth of the good Christian woman in search of our authentic selves can feel rebellious. It can make us uneasy, nervous that we're heading up a mountain of heresy rather than a valley of liberation.

Coming out from the veil of the myth exposes us more wholly to ourselves. As Erin and I shed our old paradigm of our womanhood, we became empowered to cut loose the restraints on our authentic selves. This then, became our heresy. Heretics by their very nature are at odds with established religious order.

My friend Kathy Escobar blogged a manifesto of her heretical values. Here are a few:

- If holding that women should be fully equal with men and free to lead fully and completely in whatever way God is calling them to lead makes me a heretic, then yep, I guess I am.

- If valuing practicing the ways of Jesus over nitpicking about doctrine makes me a heretic, then yep, I guess I am.

- If being convinced that it's possible that men and women can be true brothers and sisters and soul friends without all kinds of sexual weirdness and fear makes me a heretic, then yep, I guess I am.

- If loving and valuing the Bible without making it more important than the wild-and-mysterious-Holy-Spirit-at-work-in-people's-lives makes me a heretic, then yep, I guess I am.[115]

What I love about this writing of Kathy's is the veracity of her convictions. She doesn't hold back telling the world exactly what she thinks. She is uninhibited, a liberated woman free from the myth of the good Christian woman. She is bravely authentic, fully embracing her inner heretic. I am inspired.

Authentic women are natural and open. There is an absence of playacting the part of the good Christian woman. The authentic woman displays her opinions and doubts, her flaws and weaknesses, as well as her strengths and leadership. She is courageous, for it takes courage to go against the grain of the holy precepts of submission and subservience.

~~

I love being a woman. I come from a long line of women. I love the world of women that has been mine since the beginning of my days. I even have women tattooed on my body.

While I was still a cleaning woman, I asked a tattoo artist to draw up a pin-up girl depicted as a housecleaner. "And give her some tattoos," I said, "Make her curvy and sexy, but not a hoochie mama." I adore vintage pin-up girl images. These women have dangerous curves busting out all over with nary a diet in sight.

The tattoo artist created just the kind of image I was looking for. My cleaning woman pin-up girl, whom I named Rita Mae before the blood had even dried, is a sassy looking black-curled woman with sparkle in her green-inked eyes and a dose of va-voom in her voluptuous figure.

Rita Mae is an eye pleaser with her bountiful twin girls peeking out just a bit from beneath her red polka dot apron. With a feather duster in one hand, and a mop in the other—and wearing adorable red babyjane shoes—Rita Mae is one of my favorite tattoos. It's homage to the eight years I worked as an independent cleaning woman as well as a shout-out to the pin-up girls of yesteryear.

"Your tattoo offends me," said a twenty-something woman at a party I was at.

"Which one?" I quipped back as I have tattoos scattered up and down both arms.

"The cleaning woman. I don't like seeing women portrayed this way."

"In what way?" I pressed, wanting to draw it out of her. I knew what she was getting at, but I wanted to hear her say it.

"Women in subservient roles! Why do people think women always have to be the one cooking and cleaning? It's not like we automatically should be cleaning up everybody's messes just because we're female. How could you put that on your body?"

"I can see why you think of my tattoo that way, but what you don't know is that I am a professional cleaning woman. This image is about me and my work," I said as she continued to stare at Rita Mae who poses from the backside of my arm.

"Well, I still don't like it," she said. "It sends a bad message."

I wondered afterwards if she was right. Was Rita Mae sending the wrong message? Was this a reinforcement of patriarchal assigned gender roles with women always in positions of service?

Gender roles will do that. Cultural conditioning, including church culture, contributes to shaping who we are. Expectations of someone else's idea of who I am and how I ought to be can stifle the real me.

I tried hard to follow Jesus with my pleading prayers for him to transform me into a better person, into a good Christian woman. I was chasing a myth and praying for heaven to help me catch her. But I never did. Instead, I caught myself. Being me is the best fitting role I could ever imagine. I am not a good Christian woman. I am a Christ following human being, a unique individual with customized features that are all my own. I have been made in the image of God, my singular life a sliver of the grandness of who God is and what God is like. My femaleness is a part of me, but it is not all of me. I do not have to conform to the image of a good Christian woman; I want to instead, conform to the image of Christ.

Jesus was not a good Christian woman either.

I recently stumbled upon an essay from Harriet Taylor Mill, a women's rights advocate from the late 1800's who writes so eloquently about the freedom of being human:

> We deny the right of any portion of the species to decide for another portion, or any individual for another individual, what is and what is not their "proper sphere." The proper sphere for all human beings is the largest and highest which they are able to attain to. What this is cannot be ascertained without complete liberty of choice.[116]

What she writes here about proper spheres resonates with me about the sphere of the Christian religion and church. This is what good Christian women are told, that we are to hold fast to our sphere, to our space as the subservient half of the humankind. Christian women are continually reminded in all manner of ways to mind our station in life. To abandon the role of the good Christian woman (who is compliant, quiet and untroublesome) is to forsake biblical womanhood. There is an ominous inference that women who attempt to do what is meant for men alone, risk abandoning a right relationship with God and also with others.

When a woman begins to liberate herself from the myth of the good Christian woman, there's likely to be a certain amount of anger or even rage. I remember a friend of mine lamenting all the years she had let pass her by without pursuing her pastoral calling. "I thought I was crazy for wanting to be a pastor, that it was a wrong desire. I had no idea until I was in my forties that it was legitimate," she said. "I was angry at myself for thinking less of myself, and outraged at the church for teaching me to think it. My relationship with the body of Christ almost didn't survive."

Sue Monk Kidd describes her process with anger when she faced off the lifetime of oppression she had endured:

> Back during my awakening I'd learned to recognize my anger and allow it to have its place. I had stopped treating injustice against half the human population as a misdemeanor. Inside of me there had been a firestorm, and it had needed to be there for a while. It had opened my eyes, seared my heart, ignited my passion, and steepened my fierceness...At the core of the feminine wound is betrayal. [117]

That betrayal has to be acknowledged. The church of the living God has betrayed its daughters every time it relegates women to the margins. This is not representative of the kingdom of God which is a kingdom of justice and equality. When a woman realizes she has been duped, she is entitled, at least for a little while, to be pissed off. As women of faith we need to resist the temptation to quench that fire of outrage too soon. We have to let ourselves as well as one another sort out the anger.

A woman's anger needs time to flow and also to cool down. It can be compared to volcanic lava, which becomes shiny black obsidian rock once it's cooled. Obsidian is often used for sharp instruments like arrowheads and scalpels. I think a woman's fury, when processed and allowed to run its course, can become a scalpel that cuts through the inequality in her life and in the lives around her.

Anger can be creative. In her book, Sue Monk Kidd recounts a story of a group of Norwegian women skiers known as the *Kjerringsleppet*, who let their anger empower them to action:

> The group formed back in 1989 when only men were invited to participate in the opening ceremony of Norway's Alpine Center. The women felt insulted and excluded, so these thirty-five banded together, waited in the woods until the appropriate moment, then shocked everyone by swooping out of the trees on snow skis, clanging cow bells and crashing the ceremony. The country loved it, and the women became a fond symbol, so much so they were invited to the Olympics... They (learned) surprising ways to invite themselves.[118]

I love this picture of women letting their anger become a creative act of resistance. These women broke all kinds of protocol insisting they be present and they be heard. They didn't wait to be invited or given permission. They found a way and made it so.

I read a blog post online by a popular Christian woman author who was addressing the issue of misogyny in the church and a woman's anger. She gave some great points on how anger can make a person ineffective in dialog and communication. I agree with her. Anger can become destructive and muddy up the way we speak and the attitudes in which we speak. Anger can be like a loud clanging gong that accomplishes nothing except giving people a headache. But as I read her writing, I couldn't help but think of these Norwegian women skiers and their cowbells. I left this comment at her blog:

I am so pleased that the rhetoric concerning the injustice of inequity of women in the modern church is heating up. Some voices will necessarily be more diplomatic in tone, while others, fiercer. Some folks will listen to a kinder, gentler message while still others won't hear or be heard unless they act up a bit. Audience matters. We can only speak as effectively as whom we're trying to communicate with can hear us. Your post reminds me that it will take a symphony of voices to raise the message of gender equality to a resounding crescendo. Some play the flute and violin, while others beat drums and blast trumpets. Together we are making a new song for the whole world of church to hear.

It takes all kinds of instruments to make music just as it takes all kinds of voices to rise together in prophetic utterance the need for women to be free rather than a mythical version of ourselves. One of the amazing things about this is that when women live out the story that is meant to be ours, men will become more empowered to live out their story more fully, too. There is a loss among men of faith who do not collaborate with women in full equality. The absence of women from church pulpits and leadership hierarchies means half of humankind is missing. The expressed image of God is incomplete.

For God created them, male and female, in his image he made them (Genesis 1:27). Women and men together expressing the image of God.

Chapter Eleven: Unladylike Behavior

How Jesus treats women as human beings

Woman, you are freed. (Luke 13:12)

I met up with a friend of mine recently at one of my favorite Portland coffee spots. She works for a company that is only a few years old. She was so excited when she got hired on last year, especially in our recessed economy.

The company's founder and CEO is a visionary who has been committed to hiring displaced workers. He has committed to providing employment opportunities for the underrepresented, such as women and new immigrants. As a result, he has attracted a creative workforce that has helped him build his company into a thriving, viable business. Unfortunately, his string of middle managers didn't get the memo.

"When I started working, we were always being told by the owner that he wanted to help marginalized people get employed. But this is no longer happening," she said. "This company is not doing what the founder set out to do."

I sympathized with my friend asking, "Does the CEO even know what's going on?"

"I don't think so," she replied. "His original vision has become so buried in all of the policies and he's always in meetings or travelling. I wish the company would go back to following his vision."

Her story is not unique. Many visionaries set out to change the world only to find their revolution bogged down with policies, red tape and dysfunctional systems. The original intent becomes lost in the haze.

Jesus was a divine visionary who lived out a new way of relationship between humankind and God and human beings with each other, including male/female relationships. His demonstration of the kingdom of God was a vision of equality, but it has become lost in the haze of building the church. Women from all four corners of Christendom are not treated with equal measure as men. The way churches treat women does not match how Jesus treated women.

We have drifted off course of his vision of treating women with equity. It is vital for Christ followers to pay attention to the Gospel account of how Jesus regarded women. We need to take our cue from his lead.

The four Gospels provide a record of Jesus' treatment of women. Just the presence of women in the Gospel accounts is indicative of a transformed worldview. The written works of the world that Jesus entered did not feature women's voices very much. Yet all four of the Gospels feature dozens of quotes from women. Luke wrote the most pro-woman Gospel of all. Nearly ten percent of the writing of Luke has women as the source quoted in the writing, more than any of the other Gospels.[119] It may seem trivial to us today, but in that time, it was a distinctive feature of the Gospel accounts.

I love reading the stories that display Jesus' attitudes and actions towards women. One of my favorites is found in Luke. It's the account of the crippled woman healed by Jesus on the Sabbath:

> And he was teaching in one of the synagogues on the Sabbath. And there was a woman who for eighteen years had had a sickness caused by a spirit; and she was bent double, and could not straighten up at all. When Jesus saw her, he called her over and said to her, "Woman, you are freed from your sickness."

And he laid his hands on her; and immediately she was made erect again and began glorifying God. But the synagogue official, indignant because Jesus had healed on the Sabbath, began saying to the crowd in response, "There are six days in which work should be done; so come during them and get healed, and not on the Sabbath day."

But the Lord answered him and said, "You hypocrites, does not each of you on the Sabbath untie his ox or his donkey from the stall and lead him away to water him? And this woman, a daughter of Abraham as she is, whom Satan has bound for eighteen long years, should she not have been released from this bond on the Sabbath day?"

(Luke 13:10-17)

This is an astounding story in how much Jesus broke rank with religious and societal culture. In that time, men and women were separate from one another in the synagogue. But this did not stop Jesus from calling her to come out from the women's section to join him. He did this in full view of all in attendance, including the synagogue leaders. Jesus affirmed her personhood in public which put his reputation at risk.

He broke another cultural barrier when he referred to her as "daughter of Abraham." It was customary to refer to men as sons of Abraham, a gesture to their spiritual heritage, but women were not commonly addressed as "daughters of Abraham."[120] He was purposeful in calling her this when he spoke with the synagogue official, a clear indication that Jesus regarded women much differently than did his fellow rabbis and countrymen.

And then he breaks yet another protocol: he touches her. Jewish men did not touch women in public, especially holy men like rabbis such as Jesus. Jesus was turning the worldview of women as the inferior gender upside down. Jesus then healed her publicly rather than privately. In front of all to see and hear he says to her, "You are freed from your sickness." The woman instantly stands upright.

This interaction is symbolic of the healing that oppressed women of faith need. We have been bent over by the weight of the injustice of inequality, but Jesus is the Great Physician, the one who makes us whole and upright, free from shame and diminished personhood. Even within the house of God.

The church has always been meant to be like Jesus in championing the marginalized and oppressed, even when that means bucking up against the very religious system that nurtures us. This is why I call it a polite oppression. Women love our faith tribes, we long for spiritual community and a place to belong where we are free to be who we are. Jesus makes it so. The church needs to treat women like Jesus did. Imagine the outcome if women throughout Christendom began to live in the freedom of who God made us to be? Equality is a kingdom value. Jesus showed us this.

~~

One of my favorite Bible passages occurs twice in the Bible. Jesus quoted it while teaching in the synagogue one day. He said, "The Spirit of the Lord is upon me because he anointed me to preach the gospel to the poor. He has sent me to proclaim release to the captives and recovery of sight to the blind, *to set free those who are oppressed*, to proclaim the favorable year of the Lord." (Luke 4:18-19, emphasis mine)

Jesus was a freedom fighter for the oppressed and in that time, few were as oppressed as women. They lacked marital rights and property rights and were often denied educational opportunities. Women lived under a steady drizzle of derisive attitudes and actions.

In his *Daily Study Bible Series* commentaries, renowned Scottish Bible scholar William Barclay describes the station of women in the time of Jesus:

> Women had no part in the synagogue service; they were shut apart in a section of the synagogue ... where they could not be seen. A man came to synagogue to learn; but, at the most, a woman came to hear...A strict rabbi would

never greet a woman on the street, not even his own wife
or daughter or mother or sister. It was said of women,
"Her work is to send her children to the synagogue; to
attend to domestic concerns; to leave her husband free
to study in the schools; to keep house for him until he
returns."[121]

Women were clearly oppressed, their humanness demeaned and devalued
as they were judged to be inferior to men. This was the mess that Jesus
walked into, especially in the religious culture where Jewish men would
pray thanking God they had not been "born a Gentile, a slave or a woman."

A long while back I had a friend who told me that she feared that the
teaching of full equality for women would result in feminism infiltrating
the church. "It's worldly, not godly, to have women trying to be more than
God created them to be," she said to me. But it's not. A woman living in
the truth of her equality is exhibiting all who God made her to be. She
is refusing to be less than. She defies patriarchal culture and is actually
demonstrating kingdom of God culture.

The Christianized sexism that prevails in today's church is rooted
in the same patriarchal philosophy that confronted Jesus. He defied the
cultural norms of his time. He went against the grain in recognizing the
full image of God carried in woman just as much as in men. Jesus did not
treat women according to the social and religious codes of his community.

If a feminist is someone who believes women are equal with men, then
it is accurate to say, Jesus was a feminist.

Consider the woman at the well a familiar story from the Gospel of
John. Jesus intersects with this unnamed woman, a Samaritan, who has
come alone to draw water from what was known as Jacob's well (John
4:7-42). A traditional law-abiding rabbi would have had to distance
himself from her and certainly not speak to her. Her nationality was one
affront—Jews and Samaritans had a long history of bad blood between
them—but it was her gender which should have been the deal breaker.
If Jesus wanted to be culturally relevant and sensitive, he ought not to

have had any communication with her, especially in a public place like the town watering hole. Yet his treatment of this woman was informed by love instead of law. Jesus was the original outlaw preacher.[122]

His disciples are reported to "have been amazed that he was speaking with a woman" when they rejoined him at the well. They would have been familiar with the convention of the day which instructed rabbis to live by the creed that "better that the words of the law should be burned than delivered to a woman."[123]

Jesus unabashedly defied the culture of religion and social propriety by engaging with this Samaritan woman on matters of theology. In fact, his conversation with her is the longest of any of his conversations accounted for in the Gospels. And she is one of the few people recorded whom he plainly revealed his identity to as Messiah.

She returned to her community and told the men the things Jesus had taught her. Then, they sought Jesus out for themselves. The story goes on to say that the Samaritan men asked Jesus to stay in their area, which he did for another two days. The action of Jesus engaging with a woman resulted in barriers to hospitality and relationship being decimated. All because a rogue rabbi defied social convention and spoke openly with a woman.

The Samaritan woman became an evangelist to her community. Her voice became activated and she became an agent of change. This is in contrast to Jesus' lengthy discourse with Nicodemus, a learned Pharisee who sought Jesus out privately (John 3:1-21). He struggled with understanding Jesus' teaching, yet this Samaritan woman not only became illuminated, but she exhibits new found influence. This is because Jesus treated her as a human being, rather than as a woman. Her gender did not lessen nor improve her standing with him. And so, we have one of the most enduring and vivid Gospel accounts of the Son of God practicing equality. This is freedom in action.

Another part of this story that resonates with me is that the men in Samaria responded. They did not remain in their roles as patriarchal oppressors, at least in this story. They listened and followed her in welcoming Jesus and his teachings. It's a wonderful domino effect. Jesus broke down barriers to affirm the Samaritan woman, she then jumped over cultural hurdles as a woman to tell about Jesus with the men of her community. Then, these men overcame the obstacles that culture and religion had placed upon them. Everyone was committing acts of resistance of one sort or another. They did not stay put inside of their boxes.

Jesus continually resisted the injustice of inequality towards women. He rejected participating in oppressing women by devaluing them through acquiescence to the cultural norm. It was risky. What if the twelve disciples who were travelling with him decided to leave if they found him talking publicly to a woman? Jesus seemed to have thrown caution to the cold winds of oppression in order to treat other human beings with full dignity and value.

But, some might wonder, if that is the case, why didn't Jesus have any female disciples among his twelve? Jesus did have women followers. All throughout the gospels and book of Acts are acknowledgments to women who followed Jesus. Luke mentions women being with Jesus in the same breath as he mentions the twelve (Luke 8:1-3). Mary Magdalene, one of the most well known Christ followers, was given the divine honor of being the first to announce the resurrection of Jesus to the other disciples (John 20:1). She gave witness to the Savior's resurrection in a day when women were not even allowed to testify in court proceedings. But Mary Magdalene was an unrestrained woman who threw off ladylike mannerisms. Such is the birth of Christianity with a woman hailing the victory of Jesus over death.

Other women who were disciples of Jesus include the two sisters, Mary and Martha. Luke tells the story of the time when Jesus visited the two women and was teaching in their home:

> Now as they were traveling along, He entered a village;
> and a woman named Martha welcomed Him into her
> home. She had a sister called Mary, who was seated at

the Lord's feet, listening to His word. But Martha was
distracted with all her preparations; and she came up to
Him and said, "Lord, do You not care that my sister has
left me to do all the serving alone? Then tell her to help
me." But the Lord answered and said to her, "Martha,
Martha, you are worried and bothered about so many
things; but only one thing is necessary, for Mary has
chosen the good part, which shall not be taken away from
her. (Luke 10:38-42)

For much of my Christian life, I supposed that Jesus affirmed Mary
because of her submissive posture at his feet. I cannot count the times I've
heard sermons on this story teaching about worship and devotion, about
how Mary's good part was in being a submissive follower. But it is much
more than that.

David Hamilton explains that the phrase, "seated at his feet," was
a common expression used "to show the formal mentoring relationship
between a rabbi and his disciple."[124] Mary broke rank with her culture by
staying with the men, by putting herself in a place of learning at the feet
of Jesus, when women at that time were clearly meant to remain detached
from the world of men and learning. She had no authority in her religious
context or cultural context to be a rabbinical student of Jesus.

Martha defended the traditional role that women were meant to occupy.
She appeals to Jesus to compel Mary to remember her place in serving
rather than learning. But Jesus won't hear of it. He affirms Mary's choice
to learn with and among men. Jesus honored her personhood as he did
all women he encountered. Jesus lacked the sexist attitude that prevailed
against women.

Dorothy Sayers writes this:

Perhaps it is no wonder that the women were first at the
Cradle and last at the Cross. They had never known a
man like this Man—there never has been such another.
A prophet and teacher who never nagged at them, never

d or coxed or patronized; who never made arch about them, never treated them either as, "The n, God help us!" or "The ladies, God bless them!"; who rebuked without querulousness (complaining) and praised without condescension; who took their questions and arguments seriously; who never mapped out their sphere for them, never urged them to be feminine or jeered at them for being female who had no axe to grind and no uneasy male dignity to defend; who took them as he found them and was completely unselfconscious.

There is no act, no sermon, no parable in the whole Gospel that borrows its pungency from female perversity; nobody could possibly guess from the words and deeds of Jesus that there was anything "funny" about woman's nature.[125]

Nothing funny about women's nature from how Jesus talked and treated women, writes Sayers. I agree wholeheartedly. This is so important for us to pay attention to, especially those women who are unsure of their equality with their brothers. Just read the Gospel stories of every encounter Jesus had with a woman. For a rabbi in ancient Israel, Jesus spent a lot of time talking publicly and privately with women. This is because he operated from a kingdom perspective of love and justice. There was no room for patriarchy or misogyny in Jesus' worldview.

It has been pointed out that Jesus often took a woman's perspective into consideration when he taught and spoke. His teachings were constructive for women, not just men. For example, Jesus' teaching on marriage condemned the practice of men divorcing their wives and abandoning their marriage for frivolity, something that was commonplace. This left women even more powerless. Jesus' advocacy for stable marriages was advocacy for women and their welfare. He did acknowledge the existence of divorce, and then made a radical declaration in regards to it in his teaching: women themselves may initiate divorce on the grounds of adultery (Mark 10:2-

12). Women initiate divorce? This was a man's right, not a woman's. Yet Jesus sought to increase a woman's personal sovereignty and dignity.

Jesus was the great Liberator who broke social and religious constructs that demeaned women. He showed us that contrary to popular opinion, God's created order of humankind did not inherently posses nor express the dehumanizing message that one group of people had fewer rights than another. Women were to be honored, not dishonored and mistreated for the sin of being born female.

I like how Gavin Newsome, the current lieutenant governor of California, said it in the documentary, *Miss Representation*:

> When you're not treated the same, you are dehumanized. When you're not given the same opportunity, you're dehumanized. When people look at you differently because you happen to be a woman and you happen to be in a position of influence—and it's questioned—it's dehumanizing.

He's right. The cultural and religious dehumanization of women occurs every time a woman is told, "You can't do that because you're a woman. You can't preach, you can't teach, you can't have power over a man, you can't outdo your husband, you can't minister to men," on and on the list goes. It's a long list, past and present, of dehumanizing attitudes and actions that diminish a woman's value as a human being and as a citizen of the kingdom of God.

A few years ago I enrolled in a small Bible college to take some courses. The classes were very small, typically less than ten students. Discussion of the lesson was a big part of this class, something I enjoy and readily engage with. I have no problem stating my mind, even at the risk of disagreement from other classmates. In one such discussion, one of the older students, a man who was a lay pastor, had given a lengthy discourse to the class about a text we were studying. As the discussion ensued, I spoke up and disagreed with one of his points, a common enough occurrence in many classroom discussions. But he did not take kindly to this.

"Young lady, I've been around since before you were a pup. No woman is gonna tell me anything different that I don't already know. Besides, it's not proper for a woman to teach a man, especially an older man."

I sat stunned and dumbfounded with little to say. "I'm not that young," I stammered as the discussion quickly took another turn and I was left in the dust. It is rare for me to be speechless. I tuned out the class as his words kept replaying in my mind over and over again. It's not proper for a woman to teach a man. Did I just hear him say that? Strong emotion surged through me. Indignation mixed with hurt and anger churned inside of me. Hot tears welled up in my eyes, but I willed them into hiding. I would not cry in front of this man. It would only add to the humiliation that I already felt.

And that's what it was. Humiliation. I had been treated dishonorably, my personhood demeaned in front of the class for being a woman who presumed to share my point of view with a man. None of the other students spoke up nor did the instructor. I sat quietly with the bruise of being dehumanized by my fellow classmate and brother in Christ.

Once class was over I slipped out quickly. As soon as I was safely in my car, the tears I'd held back came pouring out. I drove and sobbed all the way home. And I ranted. I ranted all of the words that had been paralyzed in my moment of shame.

"What's his problem, God?" I shouted as I drove. "I'm just a woman? I can't teach him anything because he's a man? What does he think women are supposed to do in this class? Be quiet and submissive?"

As my emotions settled down and the tears dried, I began to process more clearly what had just happened. No, it wasn't me. I did not misunderstand what he said. I did not speak out of turn or disrespectfully. His issue with me was about my gender. The male classmates were welcome to engage with him in discussion, but not me.

Because I was a woman.

My voice was invalid simply because I had breasts. It shouldn't have mattered. I didn't want it to matter. Who was he? I can't even remember his name. But it did matter, because I matter. My voice mattered. My personhood mattered.

The next week when I went to class, I was ready. I was prayed up and determined to not cower back from speaking up in class—or directly to him if the discussion necessitated it—I was going to live in the freedom that Jesus had given to a woman like me. And I did, I spoke up, ready to hold my ground should his patriarchal posturing attempt to push me out of the discussion again. But thankfully it did not, though I noted that he would not make eye contact with me for the rest of the term.

The kingdom of Jesus is a kingdom of equals, where men and women can look each other in the eye and collaborate together and learn from each other. We are meant to be free together. Jesus modeled this to us in how he treated women when society and religious culture both repressed women. He did not avoid physical contact (nor likely eye), and he did not push women to the side. He invited women to be heard, to be seen, to be fully human as intended by the Creator.

Women of faith can take heart in that Jesus behaved in so many unladylike ways and inspired others to follow suit. The Mary's in his life, the Samaritan woman, the woman healed in the temple, our Bible sisters and beyond became empowered by Jesus to be free to be fully human, to have a voice and a visible presence. Even at the risk of appearing unladylike. We can be confident to do likewise as we embrace who God has made us to be and live fully in that truth.

There is no place in the way of Jesus for inequality to remain unchallenged. The kingdom of God is a kingdom of justice for it is a kingdom of love and goodness. We need Jesus' daring spirit that defies oppression in favor of equality, for love and justice will trump theology every time.

Conclusion

Unladylike: Resisting the injustice of inequality in the church

> After the illusions are gone, after a woman wakes up, after she
> has become grounded in a new way and experienced healing and
> forgiveness, she continues on with her spiritual life, investing in
> church if she chooses, but doing so with a world of difference. Now
> she can bring to it a whole new consciousness. She has a new heart, a
> new vision, new soul, new voice, new knowing and new grit. She has
> a whole new dance.
>
> Some women say you must stay in the institution and try to change
> it. Others say women cannot stay in without being co-opted, that we
> can change things best remaining outside it. I say each woman must
> do what her heart tells her.[126]
>
> Sue Monk Kidd, *The Dance of the Dissident Daughter*

In the 19th century lived the Grimke sisters, two women activist writers
who opposed slavery despite their southern upbringing. Angelina and Sarah
Grimke became fiery abolitionists in a time when there existed Christian
churches that defended the practice of American slavery. Angelina wrote a
pamphlet, "*An Appeal to the Christian Women of the South*," to persuade
women to adopt an abolitionist perspective:

> But, perhaps you will be ready to query, why appeal to
> women on this subject? We do not make the law which

perpetuates slavery. No legislative power is vested in us; we can do nothing to overthrow the system, even if we wished to do so. To this I reply, I know you do not make the laws, but I also know that you are the wives and mothers, the sisters and daughters of those who do... *127*

These words were penned more than a hundred years ago out of a sense of outrage. Angelina Grimke would not ignore her fellow Christians who acted indifferent to the injustice of slavery. Her pamphlet called for women of faith to arise and let their lives and voices help break the yoke of American slavery.

Her pamphlet was considered so inflammatory that in her own hometown the postmaster burned all the copies.[128] But she did not back down. Instead, Angelina and her sister Sarah took their message of abolition on the road speaking to mixed crowds everywhere they went.

In the culture of their day, women were not public orators, let alone speakers who called fire down on the political and religious oppressors who upheld slavery. The clergy could not contain themselves and so issued their own pamphlet to warn others against paying heed to the Grimke sisters. They condemned "women reformers and preachers, issuing a caution regarding any female 'who assumed the place and tone of man as public reformer ... Her character becomes unnatural.'"[129] Angelina eventually became the first woman to speak to a government legislature when she presented an anti-slavery petition signed by 20,000 women to the Massachusetts legislature.[130]

The Grimke sisters are a shining example of how women can resist injustice that flourishes within the halls of Christendom. We can take our cues from this pair in finding tangible, practical ways of resisting Christianized inequality. We need not wait for something to happen. We can each initiate change all on our own.

In her anti-slavery pamphlet, Angelina gave women four ways to begin resisting the injustice of slavery in their churches and homes. She wrote:

> ... if you really suppose you can do nothing to overthrow
> slavery, you are greatly mistaken... (First), You can read
> on this subject. (Second), You can pray over this subject.
> (Third), You can speak on this subject. (Fourth), You can
> act on this subject.[131]

Read. Pray. Speak. Act. These four verbs are as relevant for today's Christ following woman as they were in the day of the Grimke sisters. Simple and doable, anyone can take steps to resist the injustice of inequality in the church.

Women and men who find themselves in a church that relegates women to helper roles and denies women equal access has to search their own heart whether to stay or go. Whatever place one decides to be, there are steps we can each take to fracture the stained glass barrier that diminishes women. We must each resist the injustice of inequality within our own sphere of influence. Like Rose Swetman said, "The issue of women in the church is not an issue of theology, but an issue of justice." But how are we to proceed?

I think the Grimke sisters gave us a blueprint for consideration.

Read. We are living in the age of the digital revolution. Besides the countless books and articles that are available to read and study on biblical equality, we also have the infinite library of knowledge known as the Internet. Read to discover the historical and modern record of the treatment of women in the church. Learn about biblical sources that advocate for gender equality. Christians for Biblical Equality is one such source. Information is power.

Pray. Jesus said to pray for those who mistreat you (Luke 6:28). Prayer for the end of the polite oppression of women in the church is vital, but we also need to pray for our own sake, to be free of a spirit of bitterness and unforgiveness. If we have been wounded by patriarchy in the church, it's important that we let go of offenses and resentments.

We also need to pray for wisdom. This is the most common request I make in my prayer life, *God, give me wisdom beyond my intellect, experiences and character.* I have especially prayed this over and over again during the many writing sessions for this book. We each need wisdom in how to respond to the injustice of inequality in the church within our own story.

Speak. Women have powerful voices when we choose to use them. In the suffragist movement of the early 20th century, there was a group determined to secure the right to vote for women within their lifetime. They spoke up against injustice and demanded the vote for women to be ratified in the American Constitution. Because of their relentless outspokenness, women today enjoy the right to vote.

Christians must do the same. We must speak truth to power whenever and however we can. Silence aids oppression. Writer Margaret Atwood said, "A voice is a human gift; it should be cherished and used… Powerlessness and silence go together." Words have power, both spoken and written. Women of faith must use our voices to speak up against the injustice of inequality, for if we do not, who will?

Act. Some women will need to take decisive action such as Jodi and Mimi did by leaving the churches they loved but could no longer abide in. It cost each of these women deeply, but to have remained within a system that stifled them would have cost them much more.

Other acts of resistance include disassociating from groups that oppress women. It might be as simple as disengaging from a Facebook page or having to send a letter to withdraw membership from a group or cancel a subscription to a magazine. I did this when I realized that a popular Christian leadership magazine I was receiving vastly underrepresented women's voices in their publication. When their representative called to persuade me to resubscribe, I informed him that I could not give money to a magazine on leadership that did not affirm women.

It is in the simple, everyday transactions of life where oppression is either fed or starved. Ordinary women of faith can nourish a new way of life, the Jesus way, which is a way of equality, justice and collaboration between men and women.

To live the Jesus way means women have to be willing to go against convention and tradition. It means women have to be willing to defy the myth of the good Christian woman for ourselves and for the sisterhood of faith. We need to help each other become more unladylike.

"Don't tell women what to do," urged one friend about this book project. "Women have to discover for themselves what their path will look like." I completely agree. I hope that by reading *Unladylike* I've provoked more than a few to consider their own story and course of resistance to the polite oppression of women in the church.

A Quick Guide to Women's Listening Parties

It's been several years since I came up with the idea of bringing women together for a guided discussion about church. I realized that there was little space made for women to talk about how the messaging of the church has shaped and informed our identities as women. I wondered if women would want to talk about these things if given a chance.

The response has been telling. Every single listening party I've organized has been well-attended. But best of all, women are learning more about themselves and what they believe through the art of listening to one another.

I facilitate these listening parties with a series of questions such as:

- What messages have you learned about your womanhood from your church or faith tribe?

- What is your theology about being feminine? Do you have a feminine image of God?

- How has your sexual identity been shaped by teachings in your church? In what ways?

- Are you called to teach or lead in the Christian church? What have your experiences been like as a woman who wants spiritual influence?

- How is your marriage affected by attitudes in the church towards women?

This is just a sampling of the kinds of questions we discuss.

My women's listening parties usually last two and half hours. Women who attend often tell me that they are encouraged and empowered and want to come back again. I began hosting them on a monthly basis wondering if women would get tired of talking about these things. So far they haven't.

Many of the same women keep coming every month, often with a friend in tow.

After a couple of years I came up with an idea to help keep the listening parties fresh. I call it *PaM talks*, an idea inspired by the well-known TED talks[132] that gives presenters just twenty minutes to give their talk.

PaM talks (which stands for the **P**ower **a**nd **M**yth of being a woman) are only ten minutes long. I determine a topic and at least two weeks before the listening party, I invite women to give a *PaM talk* on a narrow aspect of the topic. At one party, for example, the *PaM talk* theme was on patriarchy. For example, I spent ten minutes giving a prepared talk tackling the question, "What is patriarchy?" Then, I opened it up for discussion. I had asked my friends Deborah and Mimi to give a *PaM talk* as well. I asked Deborah to address the question, "Is the Bible patriarchal?" and then Mimi rounded it up by telling us how her life had been affected by patriarchy. After each talk, I opened it up for discussion. There is never any difficulty having a group of women talk when given the chance!

I learn something about myself at just about every listening party. When I pay attention to the story of another, it helps me learn more about my own.

Writer and storyteller, Mary Pipher, writes:

> Stories are the most basic tool for connecting us to one another. Research shows that storytelling not only engages all the senses, it triggers activity on both the left and the right sides of the brain. Because stories elicit whole brain/whole body responses, they are far more likely than other kinds of writing to evoke strong emotions. People attend, remember, and are transformed by stories, which are meaning-filled units of ideas, the verbal equivalent of mother's milk.*[133]*

This is exactly what happens at women's listening parties. As we tell our stories to one another, our collective womanhood exchanges wisdom and knowledge. The women who come to my listening parties and share their lives have enriched me more than any other women's group I've ever participated in. I'm convinced it's because we listen to each other's story of how faith and church has affected our self-image.

Men have recently begun to ask me when they'll be able to come to a listening party. This surprised me so much! I haven't done it yet, but I think I'll experiment and host one with men and women together. Patriarchal attitudes in the church affect men, too.

I love facilitating listening parties. Sharing our stories with one another is a transformative experience. As a facilitator of many listening parties, I am convinced that women in the church (or formerly churched) need opportunity with other women to say out loud how the churches we love and have served have affected our self-image.

Women from all over tell me they want to come to a listening party. I wish all my readers could meet in my living room! But if you can't get to my house, maybe I can get to yours. Consider hosting a listening party. We can facilitate it together. Women will come if they know about it, and believe me, they will want to tell their stories. Women need to. And we need to hear them.

If you are interested in organizing a listening party, send me an email. I would love to help you any way that I can!

Pam

pamhogeweide@gmail.com

www.pamhogeweide.com

Acknowledgements and Gratitude

It has been a long climb up this mountain in writing this book. I could not have done it on my own!

Foremost above all, I need to thank my husband Jerry and my two amazing teenagers, Rose and Jeremy, for letting me hole up in my writing cave for the last nine months. You have each been beyond patient as well as encouraging when the going got tough. Thank you! I love my family!

I also want to thank Kathy Escobar for urging me to go for it. Her enthusiasm fanned the flame for writing this book within me. I also need to thank her for connecting me to Jonathan Brink, publisher at Civitas Press. I had given up on pursuing authoring a book until Jonathan spoke into my life, and on more than one occasion! Many thanks to him for guidance and encouragement and for believing in *Unladylike*.

I want to acknowledge the wonderful women who've come to my listening parties. Your stories helped me discover more of my own. Many thanks to each of you.

A very special shout-out to the readers of my blog and online writings who have emailed me to spur me on with writing this book, I haven't met many of you, but I hope our paths will cross face to face in the near future. I appreciate all of my readers!

To the women who rallied around me over and over again during the uphill course of this writing, I am forever in your debt. Thank you to Mimi Schaper for brainstorming and editing sessions, Kim Culp for support and words of wisdom, Vivian Brocato for prayer and encouragement at just the right times, Raseny Nophaenkham for long conversations and remembering me in my writing cave, Lori Bosteder for timely words and insights, Jodi Hansen for sharing her story and passion for equality with me, Erin Word for the many java-fueled conversations, and Deborah Loyd for being my theology coach and number one fan of my women's listening parties.

Also a note of thanks to Anne and Brad Shantz for sharing their love story with me. You two are way amazing!

Special mention to Craig Spinks of Quadrid Productions for believing in *Unladylike* and for all your help with the video promos. I am so grateful.

I can't forget The Bridge of Portland, Oregon, the only church I've ever been a part of where women and men are equal. You are not only the rowdiest, biggest hearted faith tribe in the Pacific Northwest, you are also the most unladylike.

Also a quick note of gratitude for the many co-workers at Legacy Emanuel Hospital who encouraged me shift after shift about the completion of this book. I appreciate all your support.

Many thanks to those who've encouraged me to write and keep on writing despite the obstacles. That includes you Bill Dahl!

And a special shout-out to Rose Swetman who not only spoke into my life at just the right time, but for her willingness to be a part of my story. Thanks for all your support during this writing project.

There are so many more to thank and honor, but space limits me, so I'll end this with one last holler for Jim Henderson, a friend from afar who believed in my writing voice when I didn't know I had one, and who has taught me the fine art of listening and paying attention. You have taught me how to go off the map!

References and Resources

Chapter One: A Polite Oppression

1   PauloFreire, *Pedagogy of the Oppressed* (NewYork: Continuum, 2001), 47.

2   Elizabeth A. Johnson, *She Who Is: The Mystery of God in Feminist Theological Discourse* (New York:Crossroad, 1999), 6.

3   Floryence Kennedy, *Institutionalized Oppression vs. the Female* (ed. Robin Morgan: *Sisterhood is Powerful*: New York: Random House, 1970), 438.

Chapter Two: The Trouble with Being a Girl

4   Joni Wise is the founder and director of We Love Kids, a ministry devoted to serving Vietnamese youth in Cambodia and Viet Nam. For more information, see http://www.welovekids.org

5   Nicholas, Kristof and Sheryl WuDunn, *Half the Sky: Turning Oppression into Opportunity for Women Worldwide* (New York: Knopf, 2009), xvii.

6   Mary Pipher, *Reviving Ophelia: Saving Our Adolescent Girls* (New York: Riverhead, 2005), 40-41.

7   Sue Monk Kidd, *The Dance of the Dissident Daughter: A Woman's Journey from Christian Tradition to the Sacred Feminine* (New York: HarperOne, 2002), 57.

8   Lynne Hybels, *Nice Girls Don't Change the World* (Grand Rapids: Zondervan, 2005),23.

9   A widely known quote from historian, Laurel Thatcher Ulrich who has since written a book of the same name, *Well Behaved Women Seldom Make History* (New York: Vintage Books, 2007)

10   In *Half the Sky*, the authors write about the wide spread abortion of female babies since the government implemented the one-child policy in 1979 as a means of population control. With ultrasound technology revealing the sex of unborn children, couples now have the ability to choose whether or not they want to birth a daughter.

11   See http://www.international womensday.com/article.asp?m=11&e=14

Chapter Three: Second-class Citizenship

12 Edwin S. Gaustand, editor, *A Documentary History of Religion in American to the Civil War* (Grand Rapids: Eerdmans, 1982), 489-91.

13 Paul Johnson, *A History of Christianity* (Clearwater: Touchstone, 1979), 337.

14 Ibid., 338.

15 Gaustad, *A Documentary History of Religion in American to the Civil War,* 501

16 Ibid., 502.

17 Ibid., 475.

18 See http://www.jimcrowhistory.org/history/creating2.htm

19 Cornelius Plantinga, Jr, *How I Changed My Mind about Women in Church Leadership* (Ed.,Alan F. Johnson, *How I Changed My Mind about Women Leadership*: Grand Rapids: Zondervan, 2010), 192.

20 Allan G. Johnson, *The Gender Knot* (Philadelphia: Temple University Press, 1997), 5.

21 Ibid., 44.

22 Ibid., 85.

23 Raymond C. Ortlund, Jr, *Male-Female Equality and Male Headship* (ed. John Piper and Wayne Grudem, *Recovering Biblical Manhood and Womanhood: A Response to Evangelical Feminism*: Wheaton: Crossway, 2006), 102.

24 Ibid., 103.

25   Polly Young-Eisendrath, *Women and Desire: Beyond Wanting to be Wanted* (New York: Harmony, 1999), 102.

26 Brene Brown, *I Thought it was Just Me (but it isn't): Telling the Truth about Perfectionism, Inadequacy and Power* (New York: Gotham, 2008), 4.

27 Ibid., 14.

28 A woman must quietly receive instruction with entire submissiveness. But I do not allow a woman to teach or exercise authority over a man, but to remain quiet (I Timothy 2:11-12).

29 Brown, *I Thought it was Just Me*, 24.

30 Ibid., 14.

Chapter Four: Sex and Power

31   Dorothy L. Sayers, *Are Women Human? Astute and Witty Essays on the Role of Women in Society* (Grand Rapids: Eerdmans, 1971), 24.

32   Dan Brennan, *Sacred Unions, Sacred Passions: Engaging the Mystery of Friendship Between Men and Women* (Elgin, IL: Faith Dance Publishing, 2010)

33   Kathy Escobar, *Cross-Gender Friendships*, See http://www.kathyescobar.com/tag/dan-brennan

34   Ibid.

35   Wayne Grudem, *Wives Like Sarah, and the Husbands Who Honor Them* (ed. John Piper and Wayne Grudem, *Recovering Biblical Manhood and Womanhood: A Response to Evangelical Feminism:* Wheaton: Crossway, 2006), 197.

36   J. Lee Grady, *10 Lies the Church Tells Women: How the Bible has been Misused to Keep Women in Spiritual Bondage* (Lake Mary, FL: Charisma House, 2000), 73.

37   Loren Cunningham, David Joe Hamilton and Janice Rogers, *Why Not Women? A Fresh Look at Scripture on Women in Missions, Ministry and Leadership* (Seattle: YWAM Publishing, 2000), 162.

38   Ibid., 164-166.

39   Ibid., 169.

40   Sue Monk Kidd, *The Dance of the Dissident Daughter: A Woman's Journey from Christian Tradition to the Sacred Feminine* (New York: HarperOne, 2002), 15.

Chapter Five: The Bible Tells Me So {Part One}

41   The Barna Group, "*20 Years of Surveys Shows Key Differences in the Faith of Men and Women*". August 1, 2011. See http://www.barna.org/faith-spirituality/508-20-years-of-surveys-show-key-differences-in-the-faith-of-americas-men-and-women. Used with permission.

42 This is a quote from Murphy Cullen, *Women and the Bible,* (*The Atlantic Monthly*, 272, no.2, August 1993), from Kidd, *The Dance of the Dissident Daughter*, 41-42.

43 John Piper, *A Vision of Biblical Complementarity: Manhood and Womanhood Defined According to the Bible* (ed., John Piper and Wayne Grudem, *Recovering Biblical Manhood and Womanhood: A Response to Evangelical Feminism*: Wheaton: Crossway, 2006), 35.

44 Aristotle, *Politics*, trans. Oxford University, *The Basic Works of Aristotle*, Richard McKean, editor (New York: Random House, 1941), 1260A.

45 John Temple Bristow, *What Paul Really Said about Women: The Apostle's Liberating Views on Equality in Marriage, Leadership and Love* (New York: HarperOne, 1991), 6.

46 Ibid., 45.

47 Ibid., 45.

48   Ibid., 119.

49 J. Lee Grady, *10 Lies the Church Tells Women: How the Bible has been Misused to Keep Women in Spiritual Bondage* (Lake Mary, FL: Charisma House, 2000), 196-97.

50 Rebecca Merrill Groothius, *Equal in Being, Unequal in Role* (ed. Ronald Pierce, Rebecca Merrill Groothius and Gordon D. Fee, *Discovering Biblical Equality: Complementarity without Hierarchy*: Downers Grove, IL: Intervarsity Press, 2005), 310.

51 See http://www.cbeinternational.org/?q=content/our-mission-and-history

52 Julie Ziglar, See http://www.twitter.com#!ziglarwoman

Part Two: Resistance

53 Carol Tavris, *The Quotable Bitch* (Guilford, CT: The Lyons Press, 2008), 175.

Chapter Six: The Bible Tells Me So {Part Two}

54 Mary Daly, *Beyond God the Father: Toward a Philosophy of Women's Liberation* (Boston: Beacon Press, 1973), 19.

55   Sue Monk Kidd, *The Dance of the Dissident Daughter: A Woman's Journey from Christian Tradition to the Sacred Feminine* (New York: HarperOne, 2002), 49.

56   See http://www.bustedhalo.com/features/anne-rice-part5

57   Elizabeth A. Johnson, *She Who Is: The Mystery of God in Feminist Theological Discourse* (New York:Crossroad, 1999), 26-27.

58   Pam Hogeweide, *Is God a Boy or a Girl?* See http://www.pamhogeweide. com/2007/02/09/is-god-a-boy-or-a-girl/

59   Johnson, *She Who Is*, 3-4.

60   Julie Clawson, *The Feminine Side of God*, See http://www. theporpoisedivinglife.com/porpoise-diving-life.asp?pageID=386

61   R.K. McGregor Wright, *God, Metaphor and Gender* (ed.Ronald Pierce, Rebecca Merrill Groothius and Gordon D. Fee, *Discovering Biblical Equality: Complementarity without Hierarchy*: Downers Grove, IL: Intervarsity Press, 2005), 291.

62   Ibid., 291.

63   Ibid., 291.

64   *Priscilla Papers,* Vol. 24, No. 2, Spring 2010, Aida Besancon Spencer, *"Does God Have Gender?"*

65   Ibid.

66   William P. Young, *The Shack* (Newbury Park, CA: Windblown Media, 2007), 94.

67   Pam Hogeweide, Gender-Bending God the Father, See http://www. theporpoisedivinglife.com/porpoise-diving-life.asp?pageID=503

68   For the complete entry for *ruach*, see http://www.hebrew4christians.com/ GrammarUnit_Four/Feminine_Nouns/feminine_nouns.html

69   For the complete entry for *rehem* see http://hebrew4christians.com/ Glossary/Hebrew_Glossary_-_R/hebrew_glossary_-_r.html

70   Johnson, *She Who Is,* 101.

71   Ibid., 5-6.

72   *Priscilla Papers*, Summer 2004, Mimi Haddad, *"Evidence for and Significance of Feminine God Language from the Church Fathers to the Modern Era."*

73   Ibid.

74   Ibid.

75   Richard S. Hess, *Equality With and Without Innocence* (Pierce, Groothius, Fee: Discovering Biblical Equality), 87.

76   Kidd, *The Dance of the Dissident Daughter*, 138-39.

Chapter Seven: Half the Justice

77   AA Services, *Alcoholics Anonymous: The Big Book*, Fourth Edition (New York: Alcoholics Anonymous World Services, 2002), 59.

78   Polly Young-Eisendrath, *Women and Desire: Beyond Wanting to be Wanted* (New York: Harmony, 1999), 162.

79   Pam Hogeweide, *Complementarianism Sucks: Telling Women to Be Quiet in the Name of Jesus,* See http://www.godmessedmeup.blogspot.com/2008/03/complementarianism-sucks-telling-women.html#comment3434078334

80   See http://www.wikiquote.org/wiki/Desmond_Tutu

81   Sue Monk Kidd, *The Dance of the Dissident Daughter: A Woman's Journey from Christian Tradition to the Sacred Feminine* (New York: HarperOne, 2002), 34.

Chapter Eight: Breaking Through the Stained Glass Ceiling of Silence

82   Rebecca West, *The Quotable Bitch* (Guilford, CT: The Lyons Press, 2008), 167.

83   Brene Brown, *I Thought it was Just Me (but it isn't): Telling the Truth about Perfectionism, Inadequacy and Power* (New York: Gotham, 2008), xxiv.

84   See http://www.jimhendersonpresents.com/about/

85   The concept of banking education was theorized by educator Paulo Freire and made widely known through his classic book, *Pedagogy of the Oppressed.*

86   Paulo Freire, *Pedagogy of the Oppressed* (New York: Continuum, 2001), 72.

87   Ibid., 81.

88 Ibid., 83.

89 Sue Monk Kidd, *The Dance of the Dissident Daughter: A Woman's Journey from Christian Tradition to the Sacred Feminine* (New York: HarperOne, 2002), 57.

90 See http://www.womensconvergence.com. If you plan to attend an event, let me

know!

91 See http://www.theelders.org

92 Ibid.

93 See http://www.theelders.org/womens-initiatives

94 See http://www.cartercenter.org/neews/editorials_speeches/parliament-world-religions-120309.html

Chapter Nine: Resisting Resignation

95 Mary Wollstonecraft as quoted by Foe J. Johnson, *A Vindication of the Rights of Women: With Strictures on Political and Moral Subjects*, 3rd ed, London: 1796, 134.

96 *The Resignation of Eve*, by Jim Henderson (Ventura: Barna Books, due out Feb 2012)

97 A little Hogeweide family trivia: one of Harriet Beecher Stowe's great-granddaughter's married a Hogeweide. This relative is my husband's grandmother. We are big fans of Harriet at my house!

98 Brenda Knight, *Women Who Love Books too Much* (New York: Barnes and Noble Books, 2000), 106.

99 See http://www.rc.vt.edu/judaic/media.html

100 Susan Campbell, *Dating Jesus: A Story of Fundamentalism, Feminism and the American Girl* (Boston: Beacon Press, 2009), 64.

101 See http://womenshistory.about.com/od/quotes/a/Florynce-Kennedy-quotes.html

102 See http://www.brenebrown.com

103 Jackie Pullinger, *Chasing the Dragon: One Woman's Struggle Against the Evils of Hong Kong's Drug Dens* (Ventura: Regal Books, 2007)

104 From a transcript of a lecture by Jackie titled, *The Release of Women into Ministry*. See http://www.godswordtowomen.org/Pullinger.html

105 Paulo Freire, *Pedagogy of the Oppressed* (New York: Continuum, 2001), 85.

106 Ibid., 47.

107 Al Doyle, from a comment left at *The God-Hearted Sexist,* Pam Hogeweide for http://www.theooze.com/church/the-god-hearted-sexist-by-pam-hogeweide/

Chapter Ten: The Heresy of Her

108 Simone de Beauvoir, *The Second Sex* (New York: Alfred A. Knopf, 1953), 283.

109 See http://millercenter.org/scripps/archive/speeches/detail/3370

110 Dorothy L. Sayers, *Are Women Human? Astute and Witty Essays on the Role of Women in Society* (Grand Rapids: Eerdmans, 1971), 56.

111 See http://en.wikipedia.org/wiki/Women_in_the_patristic_age

112 Ibid.

113 Erin Word, *Chili All Over the Kitchen*, See http://www.erinword.com/2008/01/chili-all-over-kitchen.html

114 Brene Brown, *I Thought It was Just Me (but it isn't): Telling the Truth about Perfectionism, Inadequacy and Power* (New York: Gotham, 2008), 242-43

115 Kathy Escobar, *Yep, I Guess I'm a Heretic.* You can read Kathy's entire list of heretical values at http://www.kathyescobar.com/2011/11/30/yep-i-guess-im-a-heretic/

116 Harriet Taylor Mill, *Document 15: Enfranchisement of Women* (Eds, Ann P. Robson and John M. Robson, *Sexual Equality: Writings by John Stuart Mill, Harriet Taylor Mill and Helen Taylor*: Toronto: University of Toronto Press, 1994), 178-203

117 Sue Monk Kidd, *The Dance of the Dissident Daughter: A Woman's Journey from Christian Tradition to the Sacred Feminine* (New York: HarperOne, 2002), 186.

118 Ibid., 204-05.

Chapter Eleven: Unladylike Behavior

119 Loren Cunningham, David Joe Hamilton and Janice Rogers, *Why Not Women? A Fresh Look at Scripture on Women in Missions, Ministry and Leadership* (Seattle: YWAM Publishing, 2000), from the endnotes, 256.

120 Ibid., 119.

121 William Barclay, *The Daily Bible Study Series: The Letters to Timothy, Titus, and Philemon* (Philadelphia: Westminister Press, 1975), 66-67.

122 I want to give a shout-out to the rough and rowdy crew known as Outlaw Preachers who live by grace on the wrong side of the law. Find them online at http://www.outlawpreachers.com

123 William Barclay, *The Daily Bible Study Series: The Gospel of John, Volume One* (Philadelphia: Westminister Press, 1975), 162.

124 Cunningham, Hamilton, Rogers, *Why Not Women?,* 120.

125 Dorothy L. Sayers, *Are Women Human? Astute and Witty Essays on the Roles of Women in Society* (Grand Rapids: Eerdmans, 1971), 68.

Conclusion

126 Sue Monk Kidd, *The Dance of the Dissident Daughter: A Woman's Journey from Christian Tradition to the Sacred Feminine* (New York: HarperOne, 2002), 192.

127 Brenda Knight, *Women Who Love Books Too Much* (New York: Barnes and Noble Books, 2000), 108.

128 Ibid., 109.

129 Ibid., 109.

130 Ibid., 109.

131 Ibid., 108.

A Quick Guide to Women's Listening Parties

132 TED stands for technology, entertainment and design. TED talks are archived online and cover a wide array of topics. See http://www.ted.com

133 Mary Pipher, *Writing to Change the World* (New York: Riverhead, 2006), 11.